Somewhere Totally Else

Hans Ulrich Obrist

jrp|ringier

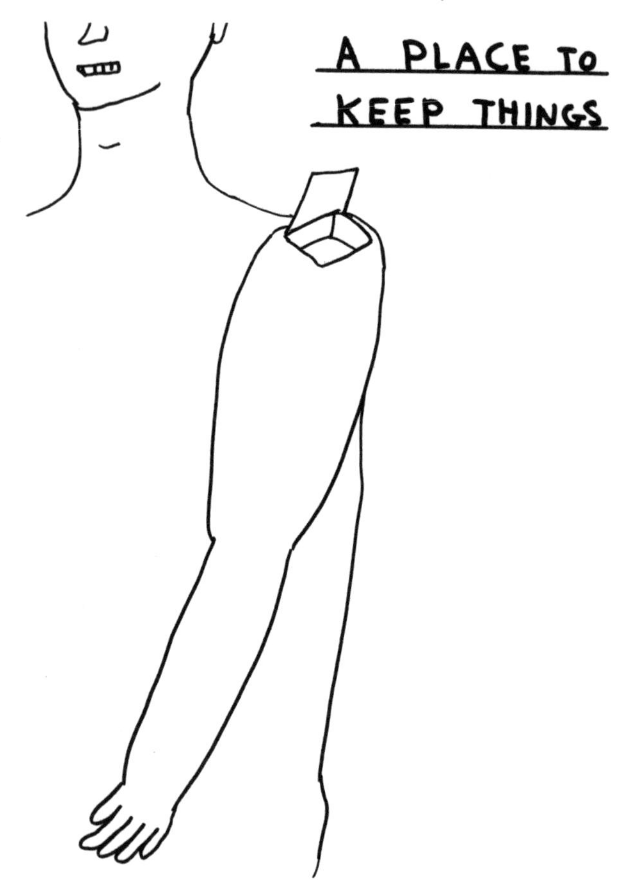

A PLACE TO
KEEP THINGS

Somewhere
Totally Else
Columns, 2012–2017

Hans Ulrich Obrist

Drawings by David Shrigley
Edited by Finn Canonica and Clément Dirié

THE PATH

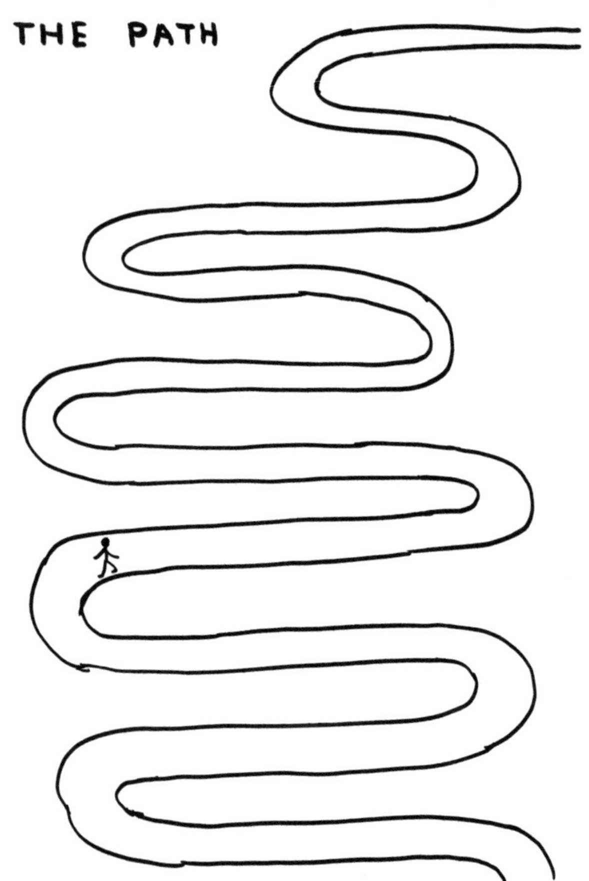

Somewhere Totally Else

Finn Canonica

There is hardly anyone more constantly involved in exchanging ideas with artists than the curator Hans Ulrich Obrist. In addition, over the past 25 years he has interviewed hundreds of philosophers, scientists, architects, and creative people. And it is part of the admirable essence and core of this great organizer of exhibitions that he avails himself of every opportunity to generously pass on all that he gains from those encounters. Hence any analysis of Obrist's work also involves all the people whose ideas and works are firmly anchored in his head. For a person who really loves art wants to impart this love, wants to arouse enthusiasm for what is perhaps its most noble task: the capacity to show us that there is always also the possibility of a different life. Or, to state it even more radically in Gerhard Richter's words: "Art is the highest form of hope." Consideration of Obrist's work, which takes the form of exhibitions, books, and his talks that occur almost daily somewhere in the world, has virtually no boundaries. The intellectual as well as the physical operating temperature of this marathon runner through the art world is extremely high. Thanks to his comprehensive grasp of art, Obrist effortlessly links art to science, architecture, poetry, and music. His pretensions are always all-embracing: there is hardly anything that fails to awaken his still childlike curiosity. Art is wherever Hans Ulrich Obrist sees art. This is certainly not to be interpreted as an authoritarian position, quite the contrary; it means nothing other than that the concept of art has become more debatable and open to interpretation—for the lay public too. In Obrist's universe everything can be connected with everything. This does not always lead to new knowledge, but it is good to keep challenging one's own mind so as perhaps to understand a little more of this art world which has long since ceased to have any geographical center, but which is organized more as a tightly woven network.

When artists talk, Obrist always writes as they do so. He calls these notes mind maps; over the years a large pool of ideas has come into being that is constantly being expanded—presumably even at this very moment. The articles assembled in this book are something like a tour around this thought structure. They were written for

Das Magazin, the legendary Swiss weekly journal where Hans Ulrich has been a columnist for many years. They do not need to be read in any set order—it is possible to open the collection wherever you like.

It is admittedly not easy to get an overview of today's artistic creativity. There is no canon for present-day art, nor are there any authorities or bodies that could establish such a canon. What the art of the present is has to be constantly debated and reassessed. Hans Ulrich Obrist's own creative output points to a way in which this can be done productively and successfully.

Finn Canonica has been the editor-in-chief of *Das Magazin* since 2007.

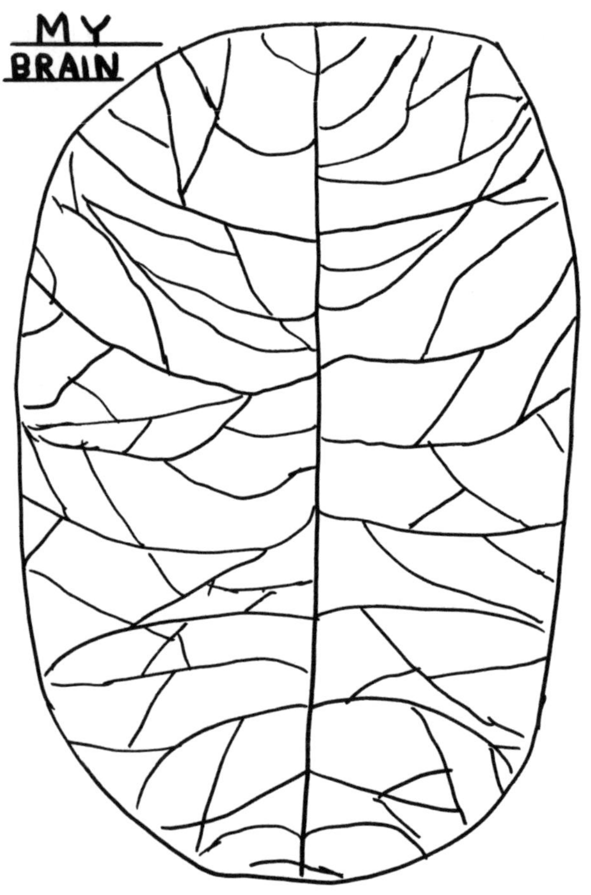

MY
BRAIN

Rituals & Rules

About Rituals

March 1, 2014

At the beginning of the 1990s when I started curating exhibitions and writing books, I modeled myself on the French novelist Honoré de Balzac, who drank up to 52 cups of coffee a day. Drinking a lot of coffee, lots and lots of it, became my first morning ritual. I regularly ordered between 10 and 20 espressos in the café. Of course, from a health point of view, that was not sustainable, and I had to come up with something else. I learnt that Leonardo Da Vinci slept for 15 minutes every three hours instead of sleeping through the night in bed. This works amazingly well. If you sleep seven or eight times a day for 15-minute-periods, you are actually never tired, and always fresh and rested. I wrote three or four books that way, and it worked far better than the Balzac method. But then I became a curator in a museum. If you work in an office, for obvious reasons it is not possible to take a little nap every few hours, for one thing because there is simply no time for it. So that was the end of the Leonardo cycle. Since then I have been practicing the ritual, if you want to call it that, of never going to bed before midnight, and getting up relatively early every morning.

The Russian film director Andreï Tarkovski said quite correctly that we lack something if we have no rituals. If we have none, according to Tarkovski, we just have to invent them. I am exceedingly fond of inventing rituals. For example, I have made it a rule to buy a book every day. I can no longer imagine a life without the daily purchase of a book. In addition, it has become a not quite daily, but almost-daily ritual to read texts by the writer and philosopher Édouard Glissant in the morning for 15 minutes. Glissant, who came from the francophone Caribbean—inhabited mainly by descendants of slaves forcibly taken there from Africa—coined the concept of "creolization." In principle this means that culture can survive only by means of constant repeated mixing with the foreign. Or in other words: by means of constantly renewed rituals.

Takeaway

March 18, 2017

One of the rituals of art is that while we may look at the works in museums, we may not touch them, far less take them away with us, for example, to look at them again at home at our leisure. It is of course right that one may not simply pop a masterpiece under one's arm. But I wanted to know what an exhibition in which different rules applied could look like. The idea came to me in the mid-1990s over a cup of tea with the French artist Christian Boltanski. In 1995, together with Julia Peyton-Jones, we put on the show *Take Me (I'm Yours)* at the Serpentine Galleries—where I now work—in which visitors were exhorted to handle the works of art, wrap them up, swap them, or even eat them. Boltanski himself contributed the work *Dispersion*, a huge mountain of items of clothing to which visitors could help themselves. The artist Felix Gonzalez-Torres was also represented, displaying sweets and posters that could be taken away.

Now, 20 years later, we have revived the idea at the Monnaie de Paris. The title of the exhibition has remained the same, some of the artists and the rules of play are the same, but times have changed. For one thing, there has been a huge commercialization of art, and the idea of free works to a certain extent takes the opposite stance. For another, the development of the Internet with platforms like Wikipedia and Facebook has led to the sharing of images, information, and music becoming a global mass movement. The contribution of the Lebanese artist Etel Adnan, who had words printed on postcards, so sharing them with the public, acts as a comment on this phenomenon. Instead of car sharing, Koo Jeong A offers a dog that you can take for walks before the next "user" takes over, Yoko Ono offers wishes for exchange, and Roman Ondák will swap his work of art for a different one—but only if you can persuade him to do so. Finally, I would also like to celebrate a Swiss artist in the show, one who already practiced artistic giving and taking 50 years ago: Daniel Spoerri cooked meals which he shared with other people, then fixed the leftovers onto canvases or buried them in the ground. In Paris Spoerri has to some extent exhumed that idea, contributing an edible marzipan skeleton that can be consumed bit by bit.

About Things We Plan To Do

January 4, 2014

For the New Year, most of us make some resolutions. We want to give up doing this, and finally complete doing that. It is the latter in particular that keenly interests me, and has done for years: unrealized projects. In every one of my countless conversations with artists, architects, scientists, and writers I ask a question about projects they have planned, but never carried out. These are divided into several groups: nothing became of many of them because they were too large in scale, for instance Louise Bourgeois' plan to build an amphitheatre, or Jeff Koons' to suspend a steam engine vertically from a crane. Others fell victim to self-censorship, while there was simply not enough money or time for yet others. A very special category of unfulfilled project pertains to architects. They are used to submitting designs they are then generally not able to realize. Many achieved a certain renown solely through these designs being made public, and became celebrated architects, although for a long time they hardly had any sizable building built. Others again, like the architects Étienne-Louis Boullée or Claude-Nicolas Ledoux working at the time of the French Revolution, produced designs the implementation of which was out of the question from the very start; their primary aim was to bring a utopian design into the world.

Sometimes I am also asked what my biggest unrealized project is, and in fact it is one that is linked to these unrealized projects. To be sure I have already introduced some in a book (*Unbuilt Roads: 107 Unrealized Projects*, 1997) as well as in exhibitions, but I would like to dedicate an enduring institution to these unre-searched products of creativity. Therefore my big project is a palace of unrealized projects. I have already asked architects for designs that—so far—have likewise remained unreal-ized. I imagine an associated agency of unreal-ized projects which would help to turn some of the works stashed in a drawer, every kind of postponed, envisaged idea, semi-rejected plan never implemented for lack of space or money, into a reality. Just like that palace some day.

What We Should Be Worried About

January 14, 2013

It is currently one of my rituals at the start of each year to devote my thoughts to a specific question. Last year it was "What is your favorite deep, elegant, or beautiful explanation?" Three years ago, "How is the Internet changing the way you think?" and a year before that, "What will change everything?" The person posing the questions is John Brockman, an author, thinker, and literary agent. Every year he asks more than 100 people in the field of art and science for an answer. He then publishes the answers on his imposing website edge.org which—something that unfortunately happens far too seldom—brings artists, scientists, and scholars into conversation with one another. This year he asked: "What should we be worried about?"

This is a difficult question. A year ago when I started writing this column, I was concerned with the writer Édouard Glissant (1928–2011). He wrote about a phenomenon that perhaps worries me most: global homogenization. We see it among other things in the disappearance of languages: of the more than 6,000 now in existence, half will have disappeared by the end of the century. We also see it in the uniformity of cities, in the global giant brands which make our centers become ever more alike. The problem with this is not an aesthetic one, but an existential one: extinction goes hand in hand with conformity.

Stefan Zweig presciently wrote in 1925: "Everything is being leveled into a uniform cultural schema ... Countries seem increasingly to have slipped simultaneously into each other; people's activity and vitality follows a single schema; cities grow increasingly similar in appearance ... more and more the fine aroma of the particular in cultures is evaporating." With globalization, this monotonization of the world has advanced much further still. But as is always the case, there is also an opposite movement: the infinite differentiation found in contemporary art. Gerhard Richter says art is the supreme form of hope. To that I would further add: Art is the best form of resistance against annihilation through standardization.

Machines that Can Think

February 14, 2015

One of my many rituals consists in answering a question at the beginning of the year that the science impresario John Brockman annually poses to a number of scientists and intellectuals. This year's question was inspired by an artist: in 1969, at the performance called *The World Question Center*, James Lee Byars asked thinkers throughout the world by telephone about the most urgent question that was currently preoccupying them. Brockman's question this time is: What do you think about machines that can think?

I try to get my head round this question while remembering the documentary *All Watched Over by Machines of Loving Grace* by the director Adam Curtis. Curtis argues that our world, increasingly determined by algorithms, will ultimately contribute less to the renewal of society and more to its ossification. As our life is increasingly recorded and made transparent, we have turned into cannibals obsessed by devouring every individual trait so that it corresponds to the general norm and thereby becomes even more predictable than before. Through the omnipresent recommendation functions on sites such as Amazon or iTunes, Curtis says, we get into a continuous loop of "If you like this, you'll like this too"—resulting in a culture which, thanks to "empathetic" personality aids, becomes not more dynamic, but more static.

The artist Philippe Parreno offers us a different perspective. He sees no threat in "machines that can think"; rather he understands them to mean programs that were written by human beings for a specific purpose, not robots which in the human sense can also follow our thoughts, and are therefore capable of empathy. This absence of a capacity for empathy that also includes an incapacity for creativity again turns calculators into a fascinating tool in art. Art made with the assistance of computers has been around for a long time already. But the "H{N)YPN(Y}OSIS" experiment that Parreno will shortly be presenting in New York really is new: an exhibition that is curated not by a human being making aesthetic assessments, but by an algorithm that has replaced that human being with the cine-image as the dominant form of the perception of time. As the exhibition also involves looking at pictures in a temporal

sequence, for him it is only logical that the age
of the thinking machine is under way here too.

The Archipelago as the Thought Pattern of the Future

January 14, 2012

We definitely need rituals, and we all miss small daily routines. That is what the Russian film-maker Andreï Tarkovski once said. For example, you may drink a glass of warm water every evening before you go to bed. I read something written by Édouard Glissant for 15 minutes every morning, that's my ritual.

Glissant was born on Martinique in 1928 and died in Paris last February [2011]. He was a writer, poet, and philosopher, but unfortunately hardly anyone in the German-speaking world knows of him. At the same time, he is an important prophet of globalization. Again and again he demonstrated how cultures can become involved in a global dialogue without losing their identity as a result of unnecessary homogenization. On the contrary: Glissant demonstrates how societies can become globalized, and at the same time even generate further differences. The alternative would of course be to become involved in the world only very little; that is the path Switzerland is currently following, having for quite some time been concerned exclusively with itself.

An important concept in Glissant is that of the archipelago, i.e. an area of sea dotted with a lot of islands, like the Antilles, where he came from. This group of islands is so important to him precisely because it has no center; there is of course exchange between the islands, but each one has been able to preserve its own culture. Édouard Glissant also wrote a novel in 1999, *Sartorius*, in which he describes the Batoutos, an imaginary people who derive their identity not from their genealogy, but from their contact with neighboring peoples. He also had plans for a Caribbean museum, a building without a cen-ter, distributed over a large number of small houses on all of the islands.

Why do I read Glissant so much? I like the idea of actually using a work as a toolbox. Of reaching into the thinking of another human being, as it were, and using individual elements as tools for one's own work. Quite irrespective of the pro-fession we are active in.

On the Night Train

March 8, 2014

When I was a teenager, I bought an Interrail pass that allowed me to travel all over Europe for 30 days for comparatively little money. I made extensive use of the offer, traveling to Paris, Vienna, Madrid, Berlin, Milan, and Rome. It was my Grand Tour, as the great educational journeys, generally to Italy, undertaken by young gentlemen in the 18th and 19th centuries, were called.

However, unlike them I had neither much time nor much money, which meant that I had only one day in each city before boarding the night train and traveling on to the next destination, because a hotel would have been far too expensive. They were marathon journeys: on a single day I had to see all the major museums, as well as meet the local artists I desperately wanted to talk to—a ritual I became very attached to, like the rituals I spoke of in my last column (see pages 12–13). The days were as full as a week. Even if I do it less often, I still always take the night train today, if I can. Not just because it is a practical means of getting about.

A night train for me is also always a kind of salon, a place of encounters. On a night train on the way from Innsbruck to Venice in the early 1990s I happened to meet Klaus Biesenbach, who is now the director of MoMA PS1 in New York. We started a conversation then that has continued to this very day; together we curated the first Berlin Biennale and the current traveling exhibition *11 Rooms*, which expands to include one more room each year. And there is nowhere I can think as well as on a night train. The idea for my first exhibition, *The Kitchen Show*, came to me on a train. With his *Station to Station* project, Doug Aitken recently demonstrated what a creative place the train is, when he invited a group of musician and artist friends, including Patti Smith, Carsten Höller, and the young Willa Nasatir, to join him on a train, and then traveled with them across the length and breadth of the United States for a month. I wrote my first articles on the train, and large sections of my first book too, because nowhere else do I feel so much on my own, detached from the world, as in my berth in the compartment or in the buffet car.

The Freedom of Limitation

June 27, 2015

In 1993 I rented a room at the Carlton Palace Hotel in Paris, and over time I invited a total of 70 artists to it so that they could do a bit of painting. It was a spontaneous guerrilla exhibition. Unusual works by Gerhard Richter, Annette Messager, and Franz West were created there. One day the visionary painter Niele Toroni turned up. He appeared with a few pots of paint and with brushes of identical width, and began to paint rectangular fields, at intervals of 30 centimeters, which produced a pyramid. With minimal means he succeeded in transforming the entire hotel. It was deeply impressive, and from that moment, if not before, it has been clear to me why Toroni is regarded as one of the most important painters by so many artists.

For a long time he has been less well known than he deserves in Switzerland, for Toroni is one of the very great living Swiss citizens. He was born in Muralto on Lago Maggiore in 1937, and first became a teacher, before moving to Paris, where he still lives today, at the age of 22.

He developed his painting principle, which he deployed at the Carlton Palace Hotel, as long ago as 1966, and he has stuck to it ever since, to this very day. *Empreintes*, prints, is what he calls the brush marks, always the same size, which he deposits at always the same intervals on a wide variety of supports such as canvas, oil cloth, or even newspaper. At an exhibition at the Swiss Institute in New York, accompanied by a show at the Marian Goodman Gallery, it became evident that this self-imposed limitation of means does not in any way lead to repetition and boredom. On the contrary—despite, or because of, the repetition of the seemingly same rectangles in a way that is always new, each work comes across as fresh and surprising. And here too Toroni has managed to change the architectonic spatial impression completely through his intervention.

You can look at the same ocean every day, Toroni once said, but you never once see the same sea. And just as the waves are similar but not identical to one another, each spot of paint likewise looks a shade different. Toroni's painting cannot be ascribed to any school or tendency. Through his concentration on one form of expression, he has taken painting to an elemental level, but by this means has also opened up a new direction

for it. As the French writer Georges Perec said:
True freedom lies in limitation.

Brutally Early

In Paris, where I used to live, there is a strong café culture. After my evening meal I often went to the Café de Flore where you would meet a whole host of people around midnight without having to make elaborate arrangements. In London, where I now live, there is no such thing. Here everything is on an even larger scale and everyone is even busier, and you have to plan weeks in advance if you want to see your friends. That is why the architect and planner Markus Miessen and I founded the Brutally Early Club, a loose circle of people who met for breakfast at half past six in the morning. We always met unprompted—for nobody has appointments at that time of day.

When I told two young British artists, Felix Melia and Josh Bitelli, about our meetings, they said half past six was the most boring time in the day. Everybody would be traveling to the City to work. Three o'clock was much more interesting, and the town was full of the most interesting people. So since then we have been meeting at 3:30 am instead of 6:30 am. We already have a new name for the morning club too: OM3am, a combination of OMG (Oh my God—my spontaneous reaction to the time of day) and three am. And we have established one rule of play: at every meeting we show the première of a film.

The first time, we arranged to meet at a branch of the Costa Coffee chain near the Eurostar terminal that is open 24 hours a day. In the middle of the night the place was jam-packed with stranded rail passengers. Because there wasn't enough space there, we moved into the station with our battery-operated projector, but were immediately expelled because obviously it is illegal to project films onto the wall of the station. We then went outside and projected the video onto passersby. The following meeting was arranged at a motorway petrol station where we directed the projector onto a tour coach, and the next time we will be meeting in a hotel at Heathrow Airport. For me it is a very nice way of seeing the city in a new light, and I like the format too. So we're a kind of cinema club only with no location and no fixed participants. And no one can claim to have any appointments whatsoever at that time of day.

About Maps

October 4, 2014

For many years, alongside physical exhibitions with real objects, I have also been producing virtual exhibitions, as on my Instagram page or in the form of books. For this purpose I approach scientists, artists, and writers to ask whether they are willing to contribute something on a theme. Recently it was on the theme of the map. Maps fascinate us because they enable us to grasp a complex thing like, say, "Europe," at a glance by means of a few lines, colors, and some lettering, and they provide orientation. With the advent of GPS (Global Positioning System) and Google Maps, the map has become completely omnipresent, as well as dynamic and more multi-layered. The maps brought together from the widest spectrum of disciplines for *Mapping It Out—An Alternative Atlas of Contemporary Cartographies* (2014) combine to form a kind of atlas of the real and the unreal world, but also of cartography itself.

The first section deals with geographical maps. Louise Bourgeois discovered a face on the map of France and draws attention to the sensory dimension of maps; Michael Craig-Martin on the other hand highlights their political dimension when he takes a map of the world and swops the names of the countries on it around. The idea that North Korea should be Belgium, Thailand Italy, and Taiwan Ireland annoyed the Chinese government for its part so much that it banned the exhibition of the work. Damien Hirst's map is more personal; on it he describes how he gets home from work. In the next chapter that is devoted to the mapping of human life, Tim Berners-Lee, the leading developer of the World Wide Web, has mapped the Internet, effectively a map by its inventor. In addition there are scientific maps that, like the atlas of anatomy, belong historically to the very early forms of site plans. The molecular biologist George Church has produced a roadmap that could be used to eliminate viruses, and the geneticist John Craig Venter a genome map of the first synthetic cell. The fourth chapter deals with maps of areas we do not know, and finally in the fifth chapter chaos is measured. What is perhaps the most moving map, drawn with a trembling pencil by Nancy Spero two days before her death, can be seen here: a portrait of heaven and a portrait of hell.

WORLDS

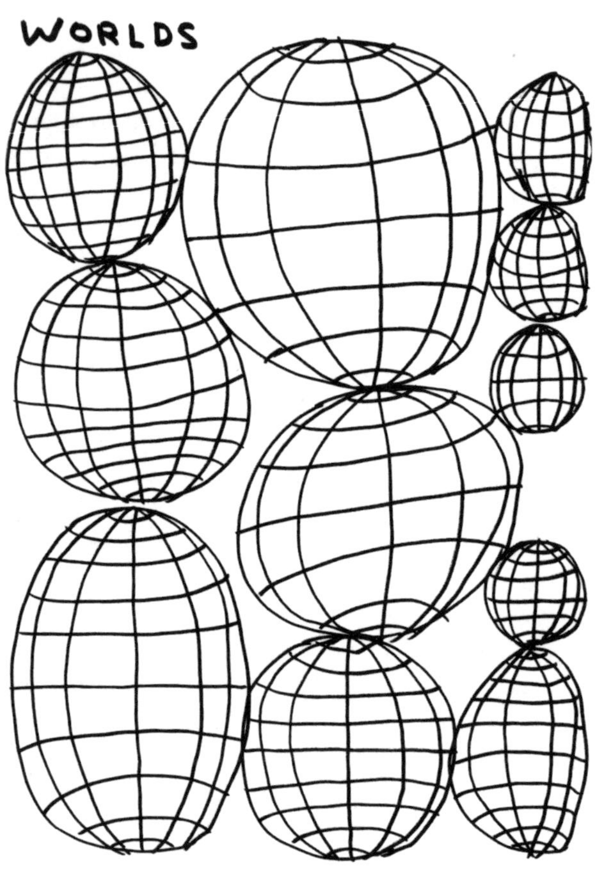

Writing in Analog Form, Reading by Digital Means

February 2, 2013

I very recently went onto Instagram. For those of you who are unfamiliar with it: Instagram is a social network like Facebook or Twitter where you can archive, process, exhibit, and comment on pictures. It is mainly younger artists who use this platform to document where they are at and what they are currently doing. Last December I was in Los Angeles where, among other things, I visited the video artist Ryan Trecartin, born in 1981, in his studio. At some point while we were talking, he took my iPhone and simply installed Instagram on it. I also already had a user name: hansulrichobrist. Only—what kind of pictures should I now show?

In 2009 I came across an article by Umberto Eco in the British newspaper *The Guardian*, talking about the loss of handwriting. Interestingly enough, Eco named neither the typewriter nor the computer as the beginning of the end of handwriting, but the smudgy ballpoint. However, with the keyboard, according to Eco, the impor-tant coordination between hand and eye is atrophying, and ultimately the specific flow of writing by hand is too. As the resistance of the pen on paper has ceased to exist, thoughts are being turned into writing in a far less restrained and less filtered way. The result is that far more is being written. I would counter this argument by saying that through email and Twitter the culture of writing in the digital age has presumably gained as much as it has lost. Even so, Eco's article stuck powerfully in my mind.

A first consequence of what I had read began in 2011 when I reverted to writing a lot of letters by hand. However, in order not to be purely nostalgic, I scanned them and sent them as email attachments. In the end this practice gave me a first idea about the kind of images I could show on Instagram. Each week since January 1 I have been asking all the artists, writers, or architects I meet in the course of my work to write a couple of sentences, which I then photograph and upload. Thus it came about that Eco's appeal to save analog writing helped me resolve my digital dilemma.

Business and
the Art Business

July 26, 2014

If artists would like to give something to society, they should also know what it is like, the legendary John Latham once told me some years ago. Only very few artists, even if they are widely traveled, widely experienced, and very knowledgeable, are likely to have any idea of how things function in an engineering firm, in the accounts department of a large company, or behind the doors of endless corridors in government Ministries and state entities. Therefore, with the objective of taking artists out of the isolation of the studio, gallery, museum context, in short liberating them from the art business and opening up new spheres to them, the British artist duo Barbara Steveni and John Latham founded the Artist Placement Group (APG) in the mid-1960s.

It was not a question of putting artists at the service of industry or politics, or of providing any kind of artistic guidance to companies; nor was the end result a work of art. The immersion of the artist in an environment that was unusual for him or her, the dialogue between the assembly line worker and the sculptor, was enough of an artwork in itself, comparable to what Joseph Beuys called a "social sculpture." Consequently, Latham was often referred to in German-speaking areas as "England's Beuys."

Ever since I was awared a scholarship by the Cartier Foundation in the 1990s that enabled me to carry out research in Paris and meet people I would otherwise never have encountered, I have wanted to make it possible for others to discover a different context too. The loose association of young artists known as 89plus (the name is derived from their year of birth) that I organize with Simon Castets has given me the opportunity to do this. Last year we were able to place two artists on the research vessel Tara, and aboard it they sailed round the world; soon there will be six of them exploring the Google Cultural Institute in Paris. Further encounters will follow shortly. What I find particularly attractive is that this project is arranged in a completely open way. Perhaps one person will merely sit around drinking coffee, but it is just then that a spark can ignite, because nothing is planned or intended. Anything can happen because nothing has to happen.

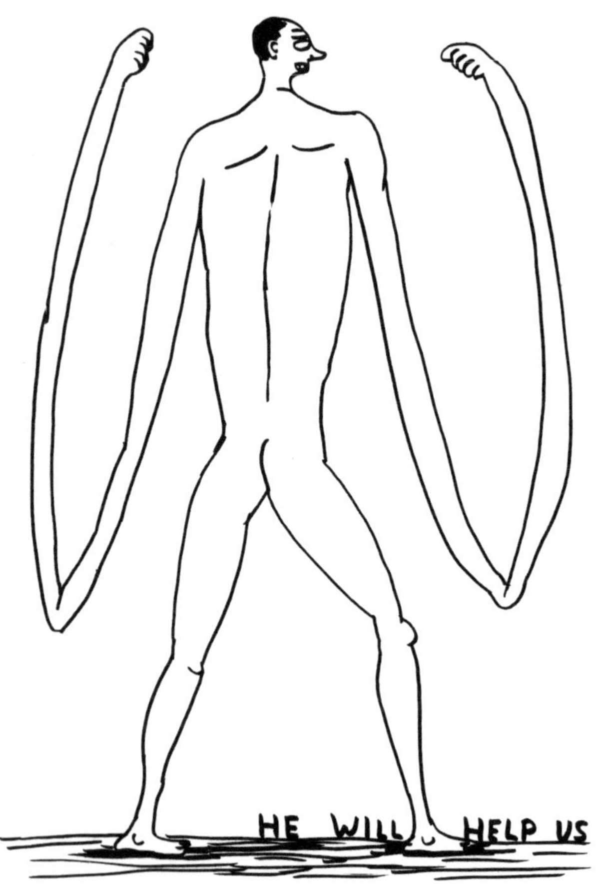

HE WILL HELP US

Luminaries

Eco and Memory

March 26, 2016

Umberto Eco died on February 19. He has been celebrated in many obituaries as a famous scholar, officially recognized intellectual and as the brilliant novelist he was. However, in remembering this centennial figure there is one aspect that has perhaps been insufficiently highlighted, and that is memory itself. I met Eco last year and interviewed him for the Venice Biennale. Toward the end of our conversation Eco came out with a sentence that fascinated me at the time, but the full meaning of which has dawned on me with all its implications only now, after his death.

We were speaking about memory. Eco differentiated between three forms: vegetable, organic, and mineral. Vegetable memory is the book—as we know, paper is made from wood, i.e. plants; organic memory is our brain; finally mineral memory has existed only for a short time. Silicon is the mineral that is contained in every electronic storage disk, and without silicon no computer can function. Eco, the man of books, regretted that organic and vegetable remembering was in retreat in the Google era, as people have found almost everything already on the Internet before they have a chance to rack their brains about it. But in external digital memory, Eco went on, people find only the public, general knowledge of the past, which he called semantic knowledge. In contrast to this is the episodic recollection of events and emotional states of our own, not public, past that nobody other than the actual person remembering can really know.

Umberto Eco's entire output can be described as a search for lost memory. As a semiotician, he took a scholarly interest in signs that are always also traces of something that was; as a writer he was above all obsessed by remembering. This is particularly noticeable in his 2004 novel *The Mysterious Flame of Queen Loana*, in which the first-person narrator reconstructs what had once been his memory in painstaking detail. Memory constantly shifts, Eco told me then. As an adult he had been barely able to understand the Piedmontese dialect of his childhood, yet in old age he mastered it fluently. The older he became, Eco said, the more he remembered. And then came this incredible sentence: "On the day of my death I will remember everything."

About Dreaming

June 6, 2015

When we go to sleep it is a bit as if we were setting off on a journey to a destination we don't yet know. In any case that's how Hélène Cixous describes it in her book about dreaming. "What a joy it is, so full of anticipation, to set out into the night," she writes, "where will it take me this time? Which country will I discover tonight?" Cixous is one of the great French writers and intellectuals. She was born in Algeria in 1937, then went to Paris; she was cofounder of the Centre universitaire expérimental in Vincennes, and the first Professor for Gender Theory in Europe. She still runs a seminar at the Collège international de philosophie, and writes essays, plays, and novels. She has published more than 60 works, on James Joyce, on Jacques Derrida—who like her came from Algeria and with whom she had a close friendship during his lifetime—and on her colorful life in the novel *Dedans*, which won her the 1969 Prix Médicis.

Not long ago I visited her in Paris, and there she gave me her book *Dream I Tell You* (2007) to take away with me. We should always write in the same way as we dream, she told me, for in the night we never tell lies. The more than 50 dreams Cixous has collected in this book are also an attempt to tell stories unfiltered, without the author intervening to make corrections. She is fascinated by this state between day and night, between waking and sleeping, this border zone in which she half consciously reaches for paper and pen and records the fragile memory. Thus she writes about a dream in which she spends an evening that goes wrong with the philosopher Martin Heidegger; in another she is confused with a woman doctor and has to assist at a birth with absolutely no experience. Of course this practice of noting down dreams reminds us of Freud's interpretation of dreams, but Cixous' dreams are more than interpretive material for psychoanalysis: they are first and foremost marvelously poetic stories.

Her book captivated me so much that I changed my life—at least temporarily. I have already tried out a lot of sleeping rhythms, the Balzac rhythm for which a great deal of coffee is required, or the Da Vinci rhythm in which you sleep only briefly and deeply without dreaming, but rest at regular intervals. Recently I have been sleeping every night for about seven or eight hours, which is quite a lot for me. While this results in less getting done, at the same time I experience more—in my dreams.

Slow Traveling

A few years ago a movement known as Slow Food got under way throughout the world. That is when we very consciously take in where food comes from, how it is prepared, and how it is eaten. Right now there is perhaps a similar trend coming into being: Slow Traveling. As a student in high school, as flying cost too much, I traveled through Europe by night train to see the artists I wanted to meet. By that means I not only saved on hotels, but I was also able to write superbly in the slowly lurching train. Some time ago I once again started using trains rather than planes wherever possible. But I'm far from being the only person to care about slowing down travel. Many artists integrate slowness into their work. Hamish Fulton for instance, who documents his peregrinations, or Paulo Nazareth who walked from Brazil to New York. Or of course there is Tino Sehgal, who steadfastly rejects planes, yet manages, as a master of overnight trains, to turn up all over the world. Together with Ólafur Elíasson and a team of engineers, he is currently developing an environmentally friendly solar plane. It won't be able to fly any faster than 100 or 200 kilometers an hour, but restricted speed is actually the point.

The riches we gain when we "lose" time are described by George Steiner in his latest essay, "The Idea of Europe," in which he analyzes European philosophy as resulting from thinkers who went for walks. Thanks to his systematic perambulations through Königsburg [now Kaliningrad], Immanuel Kant was able to penetrate the world with special precision and profundity, as was Søren Kierkegaard, because of the extensive walks he undertook in Copenhagen. But nobody has put slow traveling into words with such literary brilliance as the British writer Robert Macfarlane. In his latest work, *Landmarks* (2015), one of my favorite new publications of recent years, he devotes himself entirely to the description of landscape. This of course does not work if you roar over it in a plane, but only if you observe it attentively while walking, like him. It is a masterpiece, for the slower he goes, the more precisely he chooses his words, and the more exactly they accord with what he sees. It is also possible to draw the reverse conclusion form this: the faster we tear through the world, the more inexact, indeed blurred, we ourselves become.

The Storm

For weeks, the advance copy of a novel that I really intended to read straight away had been lying around in my house, but something always intervened. At the end of December I then met the writer Bret Easton Ellis to talk about his collaboration with the artist Alex Israel, and asked him in passing which younger author he regarded as the most interesting. The answer came quick as a shot: Ben Lerner. He had written the book, *10:04* (2014), that I had neglected for so long. As soon as I got back, I put it into my suitcase so that I could read it at home in Switzerland over the Christmas period.

The narrator is a man in his mid-thirties, a writer who had enjoyed great success with his first book, but otherwise is leading a life that isn't treating him too well. His doctor diagnoses a fatal heart condition, and while he is still trying to come to terms with the bad news, his girlfriend urges him to donate his sperm because she wants a child. Ill and overwrought, he sees one thunderstorm piling up on top of another—

as they are also above New York where he lives and works. The plot is framed by two huge storms. At the beginning one is announced, but then fails to materialize; at the end a storm hits the city with full force, as Hurricane Sandy did in 2012. The storm is not the only parallel with reality. Like the narrator, the author too is a poet and essayist who had written a widely praised first novel.

I cannot remember ever reading a book that encapsulates our time as brilliantly as this one. Great novels manage to be timeless *and* to be a monument to the present in which they are set. In Proust, technologies that were extremely modern at the time, like the telephone or the car, crop up; in Lerner, it is the atomized society of the digital age and the feeling that something completely new could begin. In anticipation of the monster storm there is a peculiar electricity in the air, an almost euphoric atmosphere that spreads to the inhabitants of the city. In view of the approaching catastrophe, all the walls of society come down. Great anarchy sets in, but fraternization between people of every condition too, and in these magic moments before the catastrophe the possibility of a different, perhaps a better society appears. In a hundred years—the work will be a classic by then—

readers will be better able to judge how accu-
rate Lerner's utopia in fact was.

The Private Lives of Trees

November 2, 2013

Last week I read a novel by the Chilean author Alejandro Zambra called *Bonsái*, like the famous variant of the Japanese garden art, which involves both supporting and impeding a plant in its growth over many years by means of painstaking minor interventions, until it eventually achieves the desired miniature form. This book works in a very similar way. It is about the laborious process of seeking, finding, and correcting a relationship; the novella Zambra develops from the relations between two people is just as small, scary, and fascinating as the sight of a bonsai.

Bonsái is Zambra's first novel. After it was published in 2006 the author, who was born in 1975, won the Chilean critics' prize and quickly became a big name in Latin America, an area already lavishly endowed with brilliant writers. The original idea for the book came to Zambra when he saw a picture of *Wrapped Trees* in the newspaper in 1998—Christo and Jeanne-Claude had wrapped up a number of trees for the Beyeler

Foundation's park in Riehen. He first went onto circle around the miniature principle in a volume of poems, and after *Bonsái*, stuck with it in his second book, another slim volume, *The Private Lives of Trees* (2010). In this, as well as in his latest novel *Ways of Going Home* (2013), Zambra has broadened out his subject matter. The patiently coddled little plant is now the recollection of the horrors of the Chilean military dictatorship. But based on the same concept, these books are like revised versions of *Bonsái*, a rewriting of it. Zambra once said he felt it was imperative constantly to revise and correct a book. He even regarded writing a book to the very end almost as an act of aggression. Indeed, a writer could not really end a book, only the reader could do so by thinking further about it, or setting it aside. Writing, he says, is like caring for a bonsai tree. It proceeds slowly, and carries on for as long as the tree is alive.

You Too Can Be Like Me

October 17, 2015

A lives in an American town, described in no further detail, with B, who in turn has a liaison with C. All three of them continually watch TV. A, who primarily feeds on sherbet, would like to become like the women in the advertisements, especially the slim Kandy Kat in the ad for a synthetic dessert. B would like to become like A, and C would like to take part in the TV reality show "That's My Partner" with B, in order to achieve the short-lived TV fame which would release him for a few minutes from his life, which has done nothing but depress him for years. That is a rough description of the level of the story line in Alexandra Kleeman's first novel, one of this year's finest new literary publications. The theme of the book is quite generally madness. Kleeman's achievement lies in giving the impression with her satire that she is speaking only of the insane and their insanity, when in fact she is describing nothing other than reality. For in this book everyone wants to be someone other than he or she is at the moment.

What is new about this is not the fact that human beings are dissatisfied with their own selves, but the fact that today the self can actually be changed, multiplied, and designed, both in the material and the immaterial sense. With social media we have the possibility of circulating a virtual identity of ourselves on the net. And thanks to the progress of medicine and food technology, it has also become possible to change our gender and our bodies. In Kleeman's book entitled *You Too Can Have A Body Like Mine*, identity optimization has become a modern fetish. Therefore the main female protagonist A, who follows a drastic diet, ends up joining a sect-like group that calls itself the New Christian Church of the Conjoined Eater. Kleeman has already dealt with food crazes and self-optimization in her earlier writings, which she published in literary journals like the *Paris Review* or *n+1*. The theme solidified into the material for a novel when she discovered an advertisement in an old comic where a ridiculously muscular bodybuilder is advertising his regime with the words: "You Too Can Have A Body Like Mine." Yes, one can indeed manage to achieve such a body. But it is less astonishing that we can do it, than that many people also want to.

The Sage of Mamelodi

August 29, 2015

I travel a lot, and these journeys are always devoted to a piece of research, a specific theme, a region, or an exhibition. But besides this I nurture an ongoing research project that comes with me wherever I happen to be. As soon as I arrive in a city, I ask: who are the pioneers here, the role models, the contemporary witnesses who have seen a whole century with their eyes? The artist Rosemarie Trockel once gave me this advice when I was still a teenager. She said: you have to meet very old people, and learn from their wisdom. Since then I have done this always and everywhere, most recently on my travels through South Africa when I asked young artists and architects who had the greatest influence on them, and had more to say than anyone else. All roads led to Philip Tabane. That given, next we had to seek him out. This was not entirely simple, for he lives in a very secluded way in a simple house in the Mamelodi township near Pretoria.

Miles Davis once called Tabane the greatest living guitarist and asked him whether he was willing to play for him, which Tabane refused to do—he did not want his identity to be lost in Davis' shadow. However, they did then appear together in the 1970s when Tabane spent a few years living in New York, and also played with Herbie Hancock and Charles Mingus. Like many great musicians, Tabane also came to Switzerland, to Montreux, and I can still remember how friends told me about the event after his appearance in 1986: about this music, which was freely improvised, was neither quite blues nor quite jazz, and had a completely distinctive sound. He always rejected categories such as Jazz, Rock 'n' Roll, or even Malombo, an independent South African Jazz tendency that Tabane created and personified. He told me that for him music-making was not a job resulting in specific products which the music business then converted into cash, leading to artists relaxing on their cushion of royalties. Rather, he himself was the music; he lived it. It came from his parents' house where his mother, a healer, freed the ill of their pains by rituals and chanting. His mother had not sought out her work any more than he had: the gift of healing had been visited on her, just as music had come upon him.

Why Kessler?

July 27, 2013

Do we need an excuse to write about Count Harry Kessler (1868–1937)? The soldier, editor, diplomat, curator, the biographer of the turn of the century, the First World War, and the Weimar Republic; the friend and acquaintance of almost all the notables of his time, who reinvented the theater and designed a model of the United Nations? No, there is truly no need for an excuse to remember this frontier-crossing all-rounder who bequeathed us a contribution to world literature in the form of his diaries. Just two years ago a new translation of part of them appeared in English published by Knopf. Since then people in Britain too have marveled at this great European who was always standing and thinking a few steps ahead of the rest of the world. Kessler was born in Paris in 1868, the son of a Hamburg banker and an Irish countess of legendary beauty—it is said that the German Kaiser fell in love with her, and had a son by her: our Harry Graf von Kessler.

Throughout his life Kessler was a traveler, and a foreigner wherever he might be. Born in France, educated in England, in Germany he was first a soldier, then a student, and eventually the defining figure of cultural life. In 1903 he went to Weimar and took over the Museum for Arts and Crafts. But for him being a curator meant not simply staging exhibitions. Not only did he bring works of art into dialogue with one another, but theater, music, and literature too, and above all people. Kessler founded the famous Cranach Press in 1913, engaging the theater reformer Edward Gordon Craig as an illustrator, and planning an ideal theater with him and the architect Henry van de Velde, who was also teaching in Weimar. Kessler was a friend of Auguste Rodin, Albert Einstein, and Richard Strauss, supporting the latter in his work on *The Knight of the Rose*. Finally he was appointed Ambassador to Warsaw, and was the companion and biographer of the progressive German Minister for Foreign Affairs, Walther Rathenau, who was murdered in 1922. Yes, perhaps there is an excuse today, when nationalism is again flourishing in many countries in Europe, and economic crisis and discord are threatening the European project, to remember Kessler, a bridge-builder and cosmopolitan.

Finely Tuned Antennae

July 16, 2016

Immediately following the regrettable decision by the British to leave the European Union, another, no less painful exit is threatening: many artists are planning to emigrate from Great Britain. Those who come from other countries are leaving primarily because of the legal uncertainty: they fear for their freedoms and their residential and work status after some of the prominent Brexit supporters had announced that if they were successful they would make life in England difficult for foreigners, or would even simply not let them in. The cities and towns of Great Britain were and are liberal, inspiring places. For all the difficulties, life is lived there according to the beautiful and correct principle that there is more to be gained from togetherness than from separatism, from mutual interest than from mistrust. However, if fear of the foreign prevails over curiosity, even a metropolis like London can lose its magic and relevance, and not only for art.

In recent times there have been emigration movements by artists, who often have more finely tuned antennae for social developments that the average member of the population, in other European countries too where national-ism, intolerance, and segregation are on the rise. We find even more examples if we go back a little further still. In recent weeks I have reread the diaries of the great cultural mediator, art collector, diplomat, and philanthropist Count Harry Kessler, driven into exile by the National Socialists. Kessler, a cosmopolitan who grew up in France, England, and Germany, and became a tireless bridge builder, contact broker, and conversationalist, suffered endlessly from the ideological barriers that disrupted the open, cross-border discourse of art, scholarship, and politics of the Golden 1920s under the totali-tarian regimes of the 1930s. In an exhibition devoted to this visionary man that can currently be seen in Berlin, it is possible to follow how, in view of that situation, Kessler predicted a dark future—unfortunately correctly. While I do not believe that the situation today can be compared with the situation then, we should nonetheless at least be on the alert.

On Genuine Dangers

December 12, 2015

In France it is current cultural practice, when major, exceptional, surprising, or dreadful things happen in the world, for the country's official intellectuals to react to them, often the very next day. Official intellectuals are pundits who do not confine their knowledge and their intellectual powers solely to the field of scholarship, but take them to the public and share them with it. This tradition is nowhere as pronounced as it is in France. One of France's foremost intellectuals is the sociologist and philosopher Bruno Latour, who published an essay that was as clever as it was provocative after the terrorist attacks in Paris. Latour wrote that the attacks on November 13, gruesome as they were, did ultimately have a clear cause that can be found and combatted, even if that is difficult. Latour sees what is ultimately the scene of the greater struggle and the real war on civilization as lying elsewhere in Paris: at the Global Climate Change Conference that ended on Friday.

Terrorists, according to Latour, would be able to make a country frightened and terrified, but would not be able to destroy our values, shake our convictions, and endanger our way of life—while climate change could. The closeness in time between the attacks and this crucial conference is therefore regarded by Latour as a greater danger than the attacks themselves—for they had led to the debate about terror that over-shadowed the debate about climate, depriving the latter of the necessary attention. Even if the conference were to result in long-term success, politics is basically inclined to tackle a short-term problem, and in the process to neglect the other much more fundamental one. Or to put it in stronger terms: it makes no sense to hunt down potential suicide bombers, but in doing so to forget that we are all steered toward a collective suicide that puts everything else in the shade. But as this is unfortunately inherent to the nature of every government, Latour writes, it is especially incumbent on citizens to make themselves heard. The destruction of the environment is ultimately "an opportunity to invent more innovative forms of demonstration than the umpteenth march from the Place de la République to the Place de la Nation".

Snow, Snow

February 2, 2016

We have to talk about the weather. I am writing these lines while marooned in a hotel in New York. Outside a blizzard is raging, it seems interminable, and the city has issued a ban on the driving of all cars. I was in the district of Chelsea on foot, and wanted to have a look at a few galleries, but because of the weather they had all shut shop; so I trudged through the streets and realized almost with fear: the sounds had gone. For a few moments in this ghostly quiet city I had the feeling that I had fallen through a hole in time, into New York before the invention of the car. I observed the thick snowflakes falling on me, and my thoughts inevitably turned to Ukichiro Nakaya. His daughter, a wonderful artist, had once told me that he was the first physicist to produce snow crystals artificially. Nakaya was born in Japan in 1900, and as a young scientist attended the University of Hokkaido. The equipment there at that time, in the 1930s, was not particularly advanced, but there was one thing that existed in plenty: snow.

Therefore Nakaya worked with what was there. He put thousands of snowflakes under the microscope and photographed them. He created a classification of snow crystals, and established such wide-ranging research around the small particles of the flake that in 1935 he opened his own Low Temperature Science Lab. A year later he finally succeeded in producing the structure of a snow crystal, as fragile as it is complicated and beautiful, artificially. Nakaya became one of the most sought-after physicists of his day; he investigated the glaciers in Greenland and the influences of frost on agriculture, and as a brilliant essayist he had the gift of explaining his subject area to a wide public. His most important work, *Snow Crystals: Natural and Artificial*, was published in 1954. Lavishly illustrated with the most magnificent forms and variants of the snow crystal, it must be the most beautiful scientific book ever to have been published.

What is more, the current snow chaos is apparently the worst since the blizzard of 1996; I was in New York then too, and remained marooned in a hotel with the artist Franz West. For a whole two days we conducted one of the most intense conversations I can remember. I'm a bit like Nakaya: snow and I understand one another.

Shame Can Save Fish

October 11, 2014

The difference between a feeling of guilt and a feeling of shame lies in the fact that in the first case we have sinned against our own conscience, in the second case, on the other hand, against the community. Shame is the reaction to disgrace, we experience it only in the presence of others; in contrast, we can feel guilty even when we are quite alone. Feeling shame as opposed to guilt has a social component: it always occurs only when the interests of the individual are in conflict with those of the group. If someone feels shame in the presence of the group, it is highly unlikely that he or she will upset it again. We could say that shame regulates social behavior by disciplining the individual through his or her suffering of the consequences. This analysis comes from the environmental studies expert Jennifer Jacquet, who for years has investigated the effects of honor and shame or disgrace on cooperation and sustainability, and has come up with some surprising results.

In her recently published book *Is Shame Necessary?* she shows how this old instrument of public morality can alter the behavior even of major industrialists, often more effectively than politics or financial considerations. Thus the US supermarket chain Trader Joe's, for example, removed all fish products that were not produced in a sustainable way from its range after environmental associations had publicly pilloried the firm. Jacquet does not argue in favor of bringing back the stocks. But she does point out that where justice and the law fail to achieve anything, public disgrace can be a means of deterring individuals and institutions from behaving in such a way as to cause harm to the majority of those around them. Ultimately, the feeling of shame is an expression of the fact that we are social creatures, in the context not only of other human beings, but of our natural environment in general. Therefore shame protects not only the group vis-à-vis the interests of the individual, but ultimately it also protects the planet.

About What Is
and What Is Not

November 15, 2014

On the occasion of the marathon I wrote about last week—an annual Serpentine Galleries event devoted to a particular theme for 48 hours—I had the pleasure of debating with the British philosopher Timothy Morton. Morton was originally a scholar of literature and devoted years to studying the work of Percy and Mary Shelley, distilling a dietary theory from it, before eventually coming to the theory of ecology and observing that it was fiercely debated among philosophers. For he introduced a new category into ontology, a field of philosophy in which attempts are made to figure out which things really exist and which do not. Morton says that between being and not being there is another third state of things, what he calls "hyperobjects" in his 2013 book *Hyperobjects–Philosophy and Ecology After the End of the World*.

Hyperobjects are phenomena of vast extent which, on the one hand cannot be seen or grasped, but on the other hand really are there and do exert a direct effect on us. One example would be global warming. Looking toward me, Morton said: "We can see Hans Ulrich, but not global warming. Despite that, it is real, for it has a causal effect on Hans Ulrich, for example when he sweats out of doors in winter." Morton evinces the same existential skepticism as he does toward all other things toward a central concept of ecology, namely nature. "Nature" for him is a social construct, wishful thinking and a normal idea that does not exist in itself, but only in our heads. But if nature does not exist, then nothing can be "natural" either, except for the things we define more or less arbitrarily as part of "nature." And from there he builds a bold, but argumentatively sound bridge from ecology to sexuality: as nothing is "natural," there are also no natural and no unnatural sexual tendencies and proclivities. And he sees yet another connection between ecological and queer theory that is more than just wordplay: a thing is never itself in all its parts, and it is therefore never "straight" (both in the sense of "unmixed" and of "heterosexual"). A frog's leg is "queer" (meaning "peculiar" as well as "homo-sexual"), part of the whole of a special kind, but it is not a frog. The frog, like all things, is thus both queer and straight.

Everything Used to Be Better. And Worse

March 30, 2013

We will never get back the world as it was until yesterday. Whether that is good news or bad always depends on how we interpret this fact. Jared Diamond has devoted a very clever book to this question of interpretation. Its title is *The World Until Yesterday* (2012) and it is a kind of summation of Diamond's research into past decades. As regards Jared Diamond, it should be said that he is actually a physiologist, i.e. a medical man, whose doctoral thesis related to the membrane of the gall bladder; he later took up evolutionary theory, engaged in ornithology, and became an established music theorist. At present he teaches geography in Los Angeles, but basically he is a sociologist. Diamond is one of the very few professors who are able to write not only scientific standard works, but also factual books that reach a public of millions. Diamond poses seemingly simple questions like: Why is sex fun? Why do many societies die out while others do not? And now currently: What can we learn from traditional societies?

In order to get to know how the world was before nation states crisscrossed it with borders, wrote constitutions in order to lay down rules, and conducted world wars in order to break those rules, Diamond visited 39 indigenous peoples in the world, many of them in Papua New Guinea; he had regularly been making research trips to that area since the 1960s. Whether it comes to dealing with strangers, with children and old people, with fear, religion, language, or food—in every area the differences between a modern state with its justice, its modern administration, and medical care, and a society living from hunting and fishing and from hand to mouth, are huge. I recently met Jared Diamond for a cup of tea when he was presenting his book in London. The greatest mistake, he told me, is to idealize traditional societies or to characterize them as primitive in a blanket generalization. There are qualities among indigenous people that are wonderful, and others that are terrible. Basically that is also an extremely apt description of our Western civilized society.

About Beaming

February 22, 2014

I clearly remember the moment when death first stared me in the face. It was when my grandfather died. I experienced the concept that he was now simply not going to be there as a huge shock—surely he had to be somewhere. So I thought about whether there might not be a possibility of finding him again. But that was only a kind of vague childish idea. Years later I met Ronald Mallett, a professor of physics, who told me that he lost his father when he was 10 years old, and only studied physics because he was unwilling to come to terms with the traumatic loss. He was determined to build a time machine in order to meet his father again. While he has not yet invented that time machine, he is still doing research into the subject today with such gusto that the director Spike Lee even made a film about it. Eventually the curator Akiko Miyake and I invited Anton Zeilinger to the Bridge the Gap? conference in Kitakyushu in Japan. It was being said that he had built a device he could use to beam, like in *Star Trek*. I will not forget how I stared at the big black suitcase he was carrying in his hand as he came into the room.

The contents of the suitcase turned out to be harmless: in no way was it possible to use them to beam objects and people through time and space. At the same time Zeilinger, a quantum physicist, has studied how it works in theory in such a pioneering way that he is one of the most important physicists working today. He was the first person to succeed in teleporting—the technical term for beaming—the quantum state of a photon across 600 meters under the Danube. Two years ago he even succeeded in sending quantum states across the legendary distance of 143 kilometers between La Palma de Mallorca and Tenerife. It has to be added that these quantum states are matterless bundles of information; therefore the technology cannot simply be applied to bottles of red wind or people without further ado. Yet when I recently listened to a lecture by Zeilinger at the DLD Conference in Munich, I suddenly had to think so intensely of my grandfather that I had the impression that in a way, beaming had nonetheless worked.

Mobile Phone Pictures
on DNA

July 18, 2015

Recently at a conference I met George Church, one of the most famous genomicists in the world. Church teaches at Harvard University and is a luminary in the field of DNA sequencing. Many initiatives in this field can be traced back to him, including the Personal Genome Project which he told me about on another occasion: the complete genome of 100,000 volunteers, linked with their medical data, is to be available free of charge on the Internet to further the development of pharmacogenetics, which could revolutionize our quality of life. But this time he told me about another idea that likewise affects us all: archiving.

Archives have long ceased to be the sole con-cern of museums and administrations—in the digital age each of us has archives to store photos, emails, text messages, and films. The mountains of data become ever more gigantic, but also less stable, because no one knows how they will last over time. Already today we often have difficulty in playing back 15-year-old data storage devices. However will it be in 50 or a hundred years' time?

Church too asked himself that question. And found the answer in DNA. If nature can manage to store several billion items of hereditary information in a minuscule space and in an error-free copyable form, then it must somehow be possible to imitate that principle, especially as the durability is unrivaled. In the case of a woolly mammoth that died 60,000 years ago, its genome was successfully partially "read out." Kept under ideal conditions—watertight, sealed in glass, and in a dark, cold place (such as Antarctica or the moon)—DNA could, according to Church, reliably store information for several hundreds of thousands of years. DNA consists of nucleic acids that are linked to form a strand. These chains of acids occur naturally, in living organisms for example, but they can also be produced synthetically. Church achieved his first storage success three years ago when he committed a book by himself, consisting of 53,400 words and 11 pictures, onto DNA. Meanwhile he is successfully archiving its multiple, but the process is still expensive and elaborate. In a few years, however, the pictures on our mobiles and chat protocols could be stored in same way as we ourselves are in our body cells.

A Theory of Everything

May 14, 2016

Recently I met up again with David Deutsch in London. I use superlatives only with great reluctance, but in the case of this man I make a half exception: Deutsch is one of the most intelligent people I have ever encountered. I also have a lot to thank him for. Primarily knowledge, but also an expression that has passed into my standard vocabulary: parallel realities. Many years ago, during our first conversation in Oxford where he teaches as a Professor of Quantum Computation, he explained to me what he means by this, using a truly martial example, the so-called grandfather paradox.

Assuming you could travel into the past, where you came across your own grandfather (before he had got to know your grandmother) and killed him—then the grandfather could not have engendered your own father, and he could not have engendered you yourself, the time traveler (who consequently, because he or she did not exist, could not travel through time either). Although time travel is theoretically possible, it therefore has a logical contradiction inherent in it. Deutsch's solution to the paradox: with a time machine you travel not only into a different time, but also into a different world. Expressed very succinctly, that is the essence of his theory of multiverses. For according to Deutsch, there is not one universe, but billions of them constituting what we call the "cosmos." Based on quantum physics, he adduces elaborate proof of this theory, which I could not begin to follow, but that is not really necessary, for Deutsch can also explain it in crystal-clear terms for ordinary mortals, as he does in his book *The Fabric of Reality* (1997). Once again I have to use strong words, and say this book has changed my life. However complex the connections that Deutsch spins between evolutionary biology and mathematics, historical theory and quantum mechanics, one senses that there are brains like Deutsch's in which everything not only has room alongside everything else, but also makes sense. His next book, *The Beginning of Infinity* (2011), is just as fascinating; in it he is no longer searching only for reality, but also for truth. He asks: What is progress? When does it stop? Where does it begin? And if it is infinite, how then can something progress at all? The short answer: every step forward is a beginning of infinity. The long answer extends over countless parallel realities.

Good Night, Sleep Well

May 16, 2015

It all began 10 years ago. The student Massimo Banzi and his classmates were looking for hardware and software in order to implement their pet inventions—robots, video installations by artist friends, or motion sensors they had built themselves. But because there were no tailor-made control systems, or the ones that existed would have been too expensive, they set about programming and soldering themselves. Their dogma was and is not to keep either the construction plans of their hard circuit boards or their software to themselves, but to make them available to all. They therefore founded Arduino; while it does earn money from its products, it does not see itself as a business, but as a platform from which everyone can serve him or herself, and we can all exchange information with one another regarding which solutions are good for which problems. Open-source is the watchword for this approach that sets out to promote the creativity of the crowd, rather than seeing it as competition.

As well as this Banzi runs a "FabLab," together with the technology designer Lorenzo Romagnoli. With its precision machines and 3D printers, such a manufacturing laboratory offers everyone the opportunity to turn their ideas into material reality—again in the spirit of Arduino, making everything possible for everyone. But because the two men do not want to implement only designs that already exist, but also those that could exist in future, they have joined forces with a specialist in this department: Bruce Sterling is an American science-fiction writer and cofounder of Cyberpunk, a literary movement that is committed to developments in the digital world, not all of which, as we know, invariably turn out positively.

So that optimal solutions can be found for the next big theme in technology, the Internet of things, the three men have linked their visionary intelligence and their technical know-how and installed a home of the future in Turin, calling it the Casa Jasmina. The Internet of things refers to objects that are interconnected with one another and with their users: mattresses that help us to sleep well, or fridges that automatically order milk. For two years here in Italy, the country of design, designers, programmers, and inventors working in conjunction with one

another are to try out ideas and objects, which
will then also be tested. Bruce Sterling has
already spent a night in the house. He says he
slept well.

PLANS

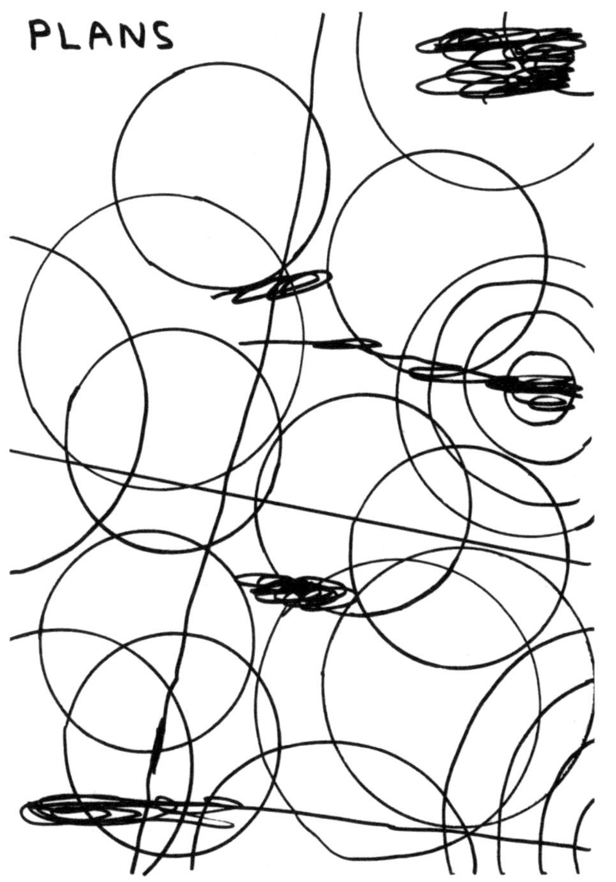

About Flying Whales

July 25, 2015

I have long acted as an artistic adviser to the Manchester International Festival, which was on again recently. On this occasion we could, for instance, once again see the various new works produced by the young British musician, singer, and dancer FKA twigs, and a joint project by Gerhard Richter and the Estonian composer Arvo Pärt. Apart from that, a hi-tech performance was announced which was said to have been produced with the aid of a technology that outstrips anything believed to be possible. The company behind this technology is called Magic Leap, and is currently constructing an instrument that could really change everything. The way we see the world first and foremost. For what the founder Rony Abovitz and his rapidly growing team have been developing for five years is a device that makes it possible to have objects appear in front of our eyes, which in the real world are not where we see them. In order to achieve this effect, they are constructing some kind of glasses that project a digital light field directly onto the retina of the eye, which consequently sees both: the real world through the glass of the spectacles, and the projected world seamlessly intervening in 3D.

The company that has collected many hundreds of millions of dollars from investors is still very reticent where information is concerned. But even so we can get a rough idea of the concept from its website: on it we see a beach with a virtual whale flying over it, but the whale is represented just as realistically as the people bathing in the sea. Or a girl opening her hands in which a small, very lifelike elephant is hidden. We can only speculate regarding the application potential of such a device. Of course it opens up a completely new dimension to computer games. But for films and literature too, a totally new field could become available, for instance if figures from novels seemed suddenly to be sitting beside you in the living room. To be able to provide a better assessment of the potential value of the hardware, the famous science fiction writer Neal Stephenson has been taken on as director of the creative department, and his job description is just as novel as the whole undertaking. Stephenson functions at Magic Leap as the official Chief Futurist.

Churchill and the Apple

October 29, 2016

Politicians and artists are more alike than might first be thought. Both solve problems, and even if in the case of one group the problems have more to do with content, and in the case of the other tend to be of a more formal nature, at the end of the solving process there is a decision— a work. Both produce reality and rely on their creativity to transform something that already exists into something different. Therefore it is not very surprising that many politicians are attracted to artistic pursuits—think of Winston Churchill—as well as many artists to the field of politics.

It was Joseph Beuys who said that every human being is an artist. For we all intervene to shape our environment. Beuys could equally well have said: every human being is a politician. In England it was John Latham and his partner Barbara Steveni with their Art Placement Group who sent artists into industrial businesses to improve relations there, and in France the actor Coluche narrowly missed becoming a candidate for the office of President—according to fore-casts, 16 percent of electors would have voted for him. Again in France, the writer and director André Malraux became Minister of Culture; the author Octavio Paz was a Mexican diplomat, while Christoph Schlingensief who died early founded the Chance Party in Germany in 2000; and finally a visual artist in the person of Edi Rama became Prime Minister of Albania.

A permanent in-between position, half politician, half artist, has been adopted by Eileen Myles, the legendary poetess. In 1991—a female candi-date for the Presidency in the United States was still quite unthinkable at that time—she too stood for the office of President and inciden-tally developed a manual about how it is possible to get to be President of America, even as a woman. Although the music station MTV sup-ported her campaign, she didn't have a chance in the US society of 25 years ago.

The preconditions for Cuban artist Tania Bruguera are just as difficult today: she wants to replace Raúl Castro as President of Cuba. For years she has been creating works of art on the theme of social and political injustice in her country. Now she wants to intervene directly and change her country as a politician. As an election slogan she has chosen the words of Che Guevara: "The revolution is not an apple that falls when it is ripe. You have to make it fall."

The Cosmic Architecture of the World

March 17, 2012

I first came across Etel Adnan's work some years ago at an art fair in Abu Dhabi. A copy of her notebooks was exhibited there. The mixture of text, signs, and drawing delighted me. I immediately embarked on reading her book *Sitt Marie Rose* (1978). What occurred then last happened to me when I came across Robert Walser while I was still at school: I read every single word Etel Adnan had ever written. I still read her work daily; it is a serious addiction.

Adnan was born in Beirut in 1925. She studied at the Sorbonne and Harvard, and taught philosophy in California. With her books on the Lebanese Civil War, such as *The Arab Apocalypse* (1989) and *Sitt Marie Rose*, she is one of the very major and important voices of feminism and the peace movement. Her name is often mentioned in connection with the Nobel Prize. We have been working closely together for a few years now. Recently she designed the latest edition of *point d'ironie*, a journal I have been editing with agnès b. for 15 years. An artist regularly creates a work in it on a double-page spread; we then print 100,000 copies, and distribute them free of charge throughout the world. She is a great artist, and one of the wisest people I have met, a living font of inspiration. A marvelous example of this is the 1986 book *Journey to Mount Tamalpais*, set in California. She saw this mountain outside San Francisco from her window, described it anew everyday, and often painted it too—as Cézanne did Mont Sainte-Victoire near Aix-en-Provence. The immaterial impact of nature is her great theme. In the volumes of poetry *Seasons* or *Sea and Fog* (2008, 2012) she talks of the air, the mist, and the sea, these hard-to-grasp things that imperceptibly influence and change us all. Our skin and our soul.

Etel Adnan always wanted to become an architect. Although she does not build any bridges or houses, her wish has been fulfilled. Whether in her poems, novels, videos (which will be available to see at documenta in Kassel for the first time this year) or painting—she is concerned with how human beings and the world are constructed from the elements of nature. I would describe her pictures and texts as cosmic architecture. And Etel Adnan as one of the greatest architects I know.

We Just Don't Know
One Another

March 17, 2012

One day after the attacks on the editorial team of the journal *Charlie Hebdo* in Paris, I had a long talk with Etel Adnan, the foremost Arab poetess, artist, and intellectual. Adnan was born in Beirut in 1925, and since the 1950s she has shuttled between Lebanon and her chosen home base in California. In the conversation she recalled a period mid-20th century, when the Arab world flourished artistically, a blossoming which was inseparably linked to a medium that has recently attracted the opprobrium of terrorists: the press. For Arab writers and poets, Adnan says, a newspaper's cultural supplement was the only opportunity to be published in the two cultural capitals of the Near East at the time, namely Beirut and, above all, Baghdad. It was only there that poems and short prose pieces were published, because Arab intellectuals had virtually all become editors in the absence of work opportunities at universities, and they tried to gain a voice for culture following this route.

Adnan herself also learnt how successfully that could work: after she had attacked the political authorities in Beirut in an article for having had the police forcibly burst into the premiere of a play and having the production banned, the government relented and lifted the ban—impressive testimony both to Adnan's voice and the status of the newspaper. But for journalists and editors like Yusuf al-Khal, whom Adnan mentions in particular, it was not primarily a question of criticism, but of making the Arab world familiar with itself, and making the East and West known to one another. For the information deficit—the lack of cultural knowledge—was in fact the greatest problem.

While her pictures exude a glowing optimism, in her poetry Adnan looks at reality clear-sightedly and with no illusions. In the cycle of poems *The Arab Apocalypse* (1989), but above all in her brilliant *Sitt Marie Rose*, she describes, against the background of the Lebanese Civil War, how it was possible for previously peaceful citizens of a country to become sworn enemies. "We speak about information and openness, but in reality two societies are living beside one another with absolutely no contact, in one and the same country," Adnan told me. "So we all speak about things of which we have no concept."

New Gossip from
the Renaissance

Over the past 20 years, during which I have met artists on an almost daily basis, I have made thousands of hours of recordings of conversations with them, now stored in my archives. A publishing house that knew of this asked me some time ago whether I would like to present the lives and work of some of the foremost artists of our day in a book. In any such enterprise it is impossible not to think of Giorgio Vasari, whose *Lives of the Most Excellent Painters, Sculptors, and Architects*, first published in 1550, is a founding work of art history, and has come to be regarded as one of the major works of world literature.

I really have no intention of comparing myself to Vasari: that would be ridiculous. But when I went back to his *Lives*, 25 years after reading them for the fist time, I was struck by how modern the book is and how much we can learn from it. Even the title is remarkable. Today we are used to considering painting, sculpture, and architecture, indeed all the arts, separately from one another. Vasari does not do this; on the one hand because the artists he is writing about, from Cimabue in the 13th century to Michelangelo in the 16th, were rarely restricted to just a single profession. It is interesting that in this way they resemble many young contemporary artists who may also be musicians, writers, directors, and web designers. On the other hand Vasari himself was not only a writer, but also a sought-after painter and architect in his day. Not many people know that it was he who built the world-renowned Uffizi in Florence. Vasari was born in the province of Arezzo in Tuscany in 1511. Before settling in Florence in the mid-16th century, he had led a checkered itinerant life crisscrossing Italy, getting to know both a great many earlier works in the churches and palaces, and most of the contemporary artists as he did so. When he came to record their lives in writing, he was ultimately able to draw on a huge reservoir of gossip and art historical knowledge. He could recount how Rosso Fiorentino trained a Barbary ape to steal grapes, but also how Cimabue released painting in the Byzantine tradition from its torpor, ushering in a period that Vasari gave its name: the Renaissance.

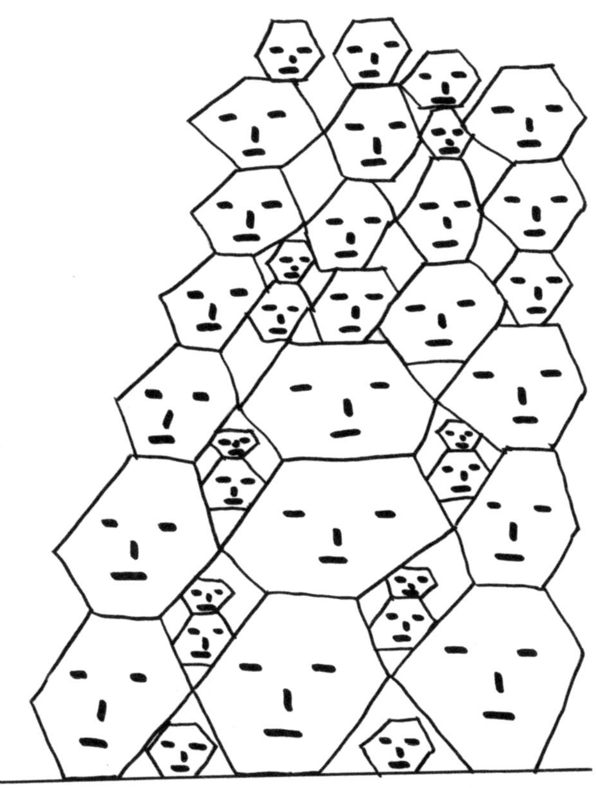

HEADS OF ROBOTS

About Names

A few weeks ago I was in New York at the house of—yes, whose house was it really? Let's begin in a roundabout way: in the 1970s he wrote a number of famous essays that provided a framework in the truest sense of the word for contemporary art. In them he coined the concept of the "white cube": the supposedly neutral white gallery space, he argued, was having such a powerful influence on present-day art that it was actually more the iconic space and less the art within it that was the truly contemporary part. We know this brilliant essayist, writer, and former art critic of the *New York Times* by the name of Brian O'Doherty. The self-same person, born in 1928, is an important performance artist and an Irish activist, who in protest at the bloody suppression of demonstrations on Bloody Sunday in Derry in Northern Ireland in January 1972, started to call himself Patrick Ireland. Like the above-named two, Mary Josephson went to study at Harvard, also in 1957: she is a splendid writer in the journal *Art in America*. The individual I met in her New York apartment is in addition the razor-sharp intellectual and bohemian William Maginn, and finally also the talented young graphic artist and painter Sigmund Bode.

The fact that the multitude of talents O'Doherty combines within himself really do not, so to speak, fit into a single name, may be one reason for his many pseudonyms. The other might lie in a certain fascination with people who multiply themselves. At least that seems likely when we read O'Doherty's latest, excellent novel, *The Crossdresser's Secret* (2014). This is about a historically documented figure from the 18th century, the French diplomat and spy, the Chevalier d'Éon. He was in the service of King Louis XV, who sent him on a delicate mission to St. Petersburg to spy on the court of the Russian Tsar. The Chevalier, who apparently had extremely androgynous features, disguised himself as a woman and was so convincing in the role that he got to be a lady-in-waiting to the Tsarina under the false name of Léa de Beaumont. But what does a false name really mean? Until the end of his life d'Éon lived alternately as a man or a woman; and at the age of 87 O'Doherty too still slips into different roles— even if he ceremoniously buried Patrick Ireland seven years ago.

Artists and Artists' Artists

January 23, 2016

There are artists who are visible to a large public and generally popular; and then there are others, I call them artists' artists, who are hardly known to the public, but are very highly thought of by other artists. Perhaps it is these artists' artists who make the deepest impression on art history. One of them is the painter Giorgio Griffa, born in 1936. I stumbled across him when I was traveling through Europe at the youthful age of 17, not so much for the sake of traveling around the continent, but more to explore the continent of art. In Italy I met the very great artists of the day: Alighiero Boetti, Michelangelo Pistoletto, Marisa and Mario Merz. And every one of them said there was one other painter I definitely had to see: Giorgio Griffa. He never belonged to any school or artistic tendency, nor did he ever complete an art training; instead he studied law and worked as a lawyer. He had a small studio in Turin. He didn't need a lot of space: his works lay stacked one on top of the other, like a pile of bed sheets.

Everything about this art is unpretentious, even the picture supports, usually simple canvases that he hangs on the wall without a stretching frame, then paints. Since 1968, the year I was born, he has been painting abstractly, and for more than four decades he has been painting stripes, lines, and sometimes numbers. There is no master plan that he is following: one stripe gives rise to the next, and if the canvas is full, he lets it dry, places it on the pile, and starts working on the next one, over and over again. The fascinating thing about this is not only the consistency of this painting, but also what the French theoretician Gilles Deleuze called the "difference of repetition": the more we see of what is similar, the more powerful the differences become, even if they are ever so small. In this quiet art it is a question of muted atmospheric shifts. We have to hear them more than we are able to see them. Next week Griffa, who was celebrated in a retrospective in Geneva last year, but otherwise rarely makes an appearance, is coming to the Engadin Art Talks. Cristina Bechtler founded these to give not only art itself an opportunity to speak, but also its originators, the artists. This year, with Griffa, my fellow moderators Beatrix Ruf, Philip Ursprung, Daniel Baumann, and I will listen with very special attention.

Abstract, Covert

May 20, 2017

Artists in the former GDR—as in the majority of Socialist states—were officially banned from creating abstract art. The non-objective was branded as capitalist, therefore decadent, which was also linked to the fact that the internationally predominant movement of contemporary art at the time, Abstract Expressionism, mainly came from the United States, and even on the other side of the Iron Curtain they wanted to be isolated from that country.

Karl-Heinz Adler graduated from the Hochschule für Bildende Künste in Dresden in 1953 and—because there was virtually no such thing as a freelance artist—became a member of the GDR's Verband Bildender Künstler [Association of Artists]. His only problem was that he wanted to produce abstract art. As he was not allowed to do so as an artist, he began to turn his attention to architectural sculpture. In the field of architecture he developed panels with simple geometric shapes that could be used to clad the facades of the estates of prefabricated houses then springing out of the ground. And this did indeed happen. The building contractor could select the facade panels as if from a sample catalogue, and arrange them on the facade himself. The result was not always a success, as can be seen in many places to this day, in Berlin for example; but where Adler himself arranged the elements, in particular in the Jena-Lobeda development, he created, almost very officially, yet bypassing the censor's office, large-format works of abstract art. He did not always get away with it unscathed. In Plauen, a town in what is now the Federal Land of Sachsen, all the facades were rehung with gray concrete panels on the grounds that Adler's panels were "a non-representational concoction thought up by the capitalist system." However, Adler did not have to fear for his job—his modular building kits which towns and communities could use to furnish their squares and parks elegantly and inexpensively had long since become indispensable. Adler constructed standardized building modules that could be assembled into playground slides, fences, and fountains using a plug-in system.

Because Adler as an artist had to hide behind utilitarian art for political reasons, he was not accorded the honor he deserved as a representative of geometric-abstract Concrete art until very late. The abstract artist who came in through the back door had to reach the age of 90 before the Staatliche Kunstsammlungen Dresden finally organized a major retrospective of his work.

The Painter in Black

July 23, 2016

"Outrenoir" ("beyond black") is how Pierre Soulages describes the sensory impression experienced when standing in front of his pictures that are always painted in black, without ever being completely black. When I met him first, he was already a mature pioneer of his subject. Now, on my second visit two decades later, Pierre Soulages is 96 years old, but still working everyday in his house south of Montpellier. Soulages designed the house himself, a cube inspired by Mies van der Rohe, surrounded by forest and the Mediterranean; not only is it regarded as one of the most important buildings of the 1950s, but under its flat roof it also houses the studio of the greatest living legend of the postwar Modern movement. Pierre Soulages, who was born in the town of Rodez in 1919, was one of the first artists from war-torn Europe whose work came to be known in the United States. New York was then the undisputed center of art, and Abstract Expressionism, with its famous exponents such as Jackson Pollock, Mark Rothko, and Willem de Kooning, was the artistic yardstick. Soulages succeeded not only in holding his own beside them, for instance with a very early exhibition at the Kootz Gallery in New York in 1954; he had also, although he too painted abstractly, found his way to a pictorial language following his own completely individual and very un-American paths.

Well away from museums and galleries, Soulages grew up in the area surrounding Montpellier. During the war he served as a farmer, and inspired by the landscape, the soil, and the tree trunks of southern France, developed his painting, characterized by shades of brown, ochre, and black. Hardly any other artist managed to be invited not only to the first documenta in 1954, but also to the second and third editions in Kassel—although his main work was yet to come. In 1979 all color disappeared from his generally very large-format and from then on always black paintings. At the same time he was never concerned with darkness, but with light. Soulages is above all a painter of light. And that is why he does not speak of "black," but of "outrenoir." What interests him is the space of light that comes into being in front of the picture as a result of the reflection on the black surface. Soulages broke away from the idea that a painting is a window uncovering a view onto something else. He conceived of his pictures as walls that hang from the ceiling, and reflect the surrounding area to the viewer, like colored mirrors.

The Great Abstract Painter

March 2, 2016

When I began to become familiar with the art world in the mid-1980s, one of my most important mentors was the Swiss curator Bice Curiger. As a teenager I sat for hours in her office that was piled full of exhibition catalogues right up to the ceiling. Her office was paradise for me—leafing through the catalogues I got to know people and works from all over the world. In 1990 Curiger asked me whether I would like to join her in curating an exhibition on Emma Kunz. Kunz had been a colorful woman, a Swiss shaman, and faith healer who made drawings with her pendulum. This interface of art with the transcendental fascinated me because there was obviously a connection there, just as Paul Klee surmised when he wrote that he wanted to make the invisible visible. In the course of research for the Kunz exhibition I came across a volume called *Abstraktion und Spiritualität* [Abstraction and Spirituality] in Curiger's catalogue paradise. And in it I found the works of a Swedish woman that are among the most amazing things that the history of art of the last 100 years has to offer.

The artist is called Hilma af Klint. She was born in 1862, studied at the Stockholm Academy of Art, but then threw all academic precepts more completely overboard than any other avant-garde artist of her time. She is the true pioneer of abstract painting—even before Kandinsky, Malevich, and Mondrian she was painting non-representationally. But not in a small, secret, and tentative way—no, she was painting enormous canvases. Central to her work is the large-format series *Paintings for the Temple*, 193 abstract paintings in which she attempts to overcome the contradictions between the temporal and the cosmic, the spiritual and the material, good and evil. Af Klint made Rudolf Steiner's acquaintance, and his anthroposophy influenced her. But her work cannot be reduced to that, for she worked quite independently and in seclusion in the Swedish forest—another reason why the worldwide recognition that is her due, on equal terms with the other major representatives of Modernism, came about only very hesitantly. A further reason can be ascribed to her herself. Shortly before her death in 1944 she decreed that her pictures should not be shown for 20 years, as the world was not yet ready for them. Those 20 years are long since past; it is now time to honor af Klint as she deserves.

Dada in Dubai

July 5, 2016

There is a lot of talk this year about how Hugo Ball and Emmy Hennings and their comrades-in-arms turned the world upside down from the Spiegelgasse in Zurich. Dada's subversive joke spread to Paris, to Berlin, to New York, and with it an art form that Dada had invented: performance. What mattered first and foremost to the Dadaist performers in this mixture of playfulness and cabaret was to do everything as differently as possible. Something less well known is that one of the great inspirers of Dada was the dramatist Frank Wedekind, who had grown up in Switzerland. I was recently reminded of this circumstance not by a Swiss art scholar, but by Hassan Sharif, a great—really we have to say, *the* great—artist from the United Arab Emirates. For Sharif, performance art starts in 1906, i.e. a good 10 years before Dada, with the first performance of Wedekind's scandal-provoking play *Spring Awakening*, which was once banned by the censors, but today is among the most widely performed and best-known plays of the turn of the century.

Sharif was born in the Emirates in 1951, and if only for purely biographical reasons must feel a great affinity to Wedekind and the Dadaists. For, like them, in his own country he met with a total lack of comprehension regarding what he was doing. For his first performances in which he used sand to heap up shapes in the desert that the wind then carried away, there was neither a public nor a name—as there was absolutely no art. Today the Emirates and neighboring Qatar are among the world's up-and-coming art hotspots: the largest art fair in the Middle East is held in Dubai every year, the superb Museum of Islamic Art and the Arab Museum of Modern Art are in Doha, the Louvre and the Guggenheim are building branches in Abu Dhabi, and the Sharjah Art Foundation puts on marvelous exhibitions, soon to include one devoted to Sharif. He has now been working for many years on a new realism by taking everyday objects from the Middle East out of context, and tying them together with string and ropes in a new way. The rise of the Emirates to become a stronghold of high culture has many reasons. But a crucial one is an artist like Sharif, who literally planted the seed of art in the desert. The fact that this seed had traveled all the way from the Spiegelgasse, is a circumstance that would surely have delighted the Zurich Dadaists.

Black Vision

December 21, 2016

While Black Music, represented by artists like Beyoncé, Kendrick Lamar, and Kanye West, has long been a fully-fledged cultural asset, it had not hitherto proved possible for the Black Movie or Black Video to become established to anything like the same extent. With the hour-long musical-cinematographic phenomenon that is Beyoncé's current album *Lemonade*, which could be described only very fragmentarily as a "music video," that could be about to change.

One of the most important inspirations for this video by the director Kahlil Joseph was the legendary cameraman and film theorist Arthur Jafa. I had met him as long ago as 2000 when I arranged for videos by him to be played on public billboards in Seoul so that they could be viewed from the car, as in an art drive-in. The movement known as BVI, an acronym for "Black Vision Intonation," goes back to Jafa. BVI's objective is to create an individual Afro-American aesthetic for the art of the moving picture. Just as after a few notes from a song by Kendrick Lamar we immediately recognize that we are dealing with Black Music, according to Jafa's ideas we should also be able to recognize a Black Video as such. He has very recently shown what such a cinematic art could look like with two music videos for Solange Knowles, Beyoncé's younger sister. In the videos for *Don't Touch My Hair* and *Cranes In The Sky* he celebrates the body, and by means of a cleverly worked out cutting concept ensures an incredibly rhythmic flow. In the world beyond music he exhibited this form of rhythmic video in an art gallery for the first time a few weeks ago with the work *Love Is the Message, The Message Is Death*, at Gavin Brown's gallery in New York. This seven-minute, intense, artistically composed picture collage, accompanied by a ballad by Kanye West, is a visual hymn to the Afro-American present.

Here too the moving body is central, but likewise the—carefully formulated—checkered lives of many black people in the United States. For, as Jafa told me in conversation, even under the presidency of Barack Obama, Afro-Americans were disadvantaged, found fewer jobs, and were more frequently exposed to police violence than other groups. Images of poverty and beauty, raw violence and tender love, pass before our eyes in this ecstatic, epic video. It is the quintessence of what Jafa means by "Black Vision."

The Laboratory

December 5, 2015

The Global Climate Change Conference in Paris is still in progress. Newspapers are full of reports on the topic, television is broadcasting documentaries about protecting the climate, and at home at supper there are discussions about the sustainability of salami. Yet soon, when the conference is over, for all that the topic is the most urgent one of the present day, it might well get lost again in the ambient buzz of current events. One person who suffers in the face of this fact and therefore is simply unwilling to accept it is Gustav Metzger. The artist who was born in Germany is now 89 years old, but still operates as an activist in the first flush of enthusiasm. He sees his existence as an artist as a privilege enabling him—favored by the resources at his disposal—to be at the forefront of the fight to protect the environment.

Just this November, along with the Serpentine Galleries, he launched the "Remember Nature" campaign, calling on artists internationally to create works for the campaign that are directed against the destruction of the planet. In parallel with that he has also set up a blog that continues to be active and to grow. But one of the most spectacular works in which he has explored the self-destructive power of humankind is the installation *Extremes Touch*, which—after more than 45 years—was again recreated for the first time in the context of a major double exhibition of Metzger's work at the Kunsthal Oslo. Now, as in 1968 in the then brand-new laboratory of the Chemistry Department of University College in Swansea in Wales, we again see in fast motion where the chain reaction that human beings with their emissions and devastation have triggered is leading. With water, compressed air, liquid nitrogen, crystalline silicates, and a stroboscope he brings the laboratory literally to the boil: water jets jingle as they hit reagent tubes, drops vaporize with a hiss on hot plates and form dense clouds, and however beautiful the way in which polystyrene blocks rise in the air as if by the hands of ghosts may be while from time to time a rainbow appears, it is also just as eerie to watch how the order of things turns into chaos in this laboratory that has gone berserk. It is the most memorable exhibition I have seen this year, and will surely leave a more enduring impression than the discussions at the Conference, however important they may be too.

The Savior of All Species

September 17, 2016

This summer I visited Gustav Metzger, as I do every year. Metzger is now 90 years old, but still a militant environmental activist who was in at the start, and he has often told me about people who have made an outstanding contribution toward saving the planet. This year he informed me that one of the most important individuals of all had recently died—Luc Hoffmann, the founder of the WWF, a philanthropist and research scientist.

I had the good fortune to have known Hoffmann for many years, a quiet, but extremely tenacious protector of nature, and an impressive human being. Hoffmann was born in Basel in 1923 where he studied zoology and became an expert orni-thologist. He once told me that it was on a research field trip that had taken him to France after the War that he had suffered an emotional shock. This was when he saw the Camargue for the first time, an area of marshland covering around 1,000 square kilometers on the coast of Provence between Marseilles and Montpellier, where the Rhône flows into the Mediterranean. There are very few people living there, but huge populations of rare water birds, some then threatened with extinction, first and foremost the flamingo. The fact that this species and the 400 other species of bird still exist in the shallow waters of the Camargue is due to Hoffmann.

As the heir to the Hoffmann-La Roche company, he had the financial resources to preserve this tract of land in all the richness of its species. Not only did he describe the reality, he also changed it. To do so he bought up large areas, and used diplomatic aplomb to persuade the French government to make virtually all of the Camargue a conservation area. He founded the Tour du Valat, a research center for the conservation of the Mediterranean wetlands, and very early recognized that while researchers working on their own could do a great deal, together they could accomplish much more. Therefore he not only set up bursaries for young scientists from throughout the world, so involving them in the protection of species, but also founded many organizations such as the International Union for the Conservation of Nature and Natural Resources (IUCN), and the World Wide Fund for Nature (WWF), which has grown to become one of the largest institutions for the protection of nature in the world. Tragically this great Swiss national died in July. As Gustav Metzger said, with him, a person who was exceptionally important for the preservation of the planet has been lost.

Millipedes

July 19, 2014

Recently, the great English author A. S. Byatt asked me the rather casual and rhetorical question: When had I last seen a millipede. This question completely shocked me. As a child I constantly saw millipedes, watching them in fascination, and of course also feeling a little repelled by them, but I cannot remember having spotted any such little creature in the past 20 years. I do not know if the millipede genus is existentially threatened, but I couldn't help thinking of the extinction of the dinosaurs, bee colony collapse, the endangered status of pandas, and the disappearance of entire species. Indeed, not only were and are biological species constantly threatened by extinction, but cultures such as the Maya in Central America, cultural technologies such as handwriting, and whole cities and tracts of land are, too, as a result of global warming and rising sea levels. I asked myself: does it have to be like this, with many valuable things being irrevocably lost in this way?

Throughout the summer I want to give myself time to ponder this, so that by autumn I hope I can come up with some results. I will be supported in this research by our team at the Serpentine Galleries and the artist Gustav Metzger, for whom the theme of extinction is a kind of leitmotiv of his life. As a child he fled from Germany to England to escape the Holocaust to which almost his entire family fell victim. As an artist and an activist he has campaigned vigorously for the protection of nature, always insisting on the question of exactly who is responsible for environmental destruction, and how those who cause it could be punished. However, punishment does not bring what has been destroyed back. At this point another pioneer of the global environmental protection movement comes into the picture—Stewart Brand—who has achieved fame through his *Whole Earth Catalog* (1968–1972). His most recent major project *Revive & Restore* is dedicated to the revival of extinct species with the help of modern genetics and technology. If things get that far, the question of course will no longer be whether we can bring dinosaurs or Neanderthal man back to life—but whether we have the right to.

For *Stockholm June (Phase 1)* (1972–2007) Gustav Metzger got 120 cars to release their exhaust fumes into a tent-like container. Within a short time the air quality becomes so poor in the container, that life and survival would be impossible for most of species.

The Dimensions of Dung

August 8, 2015

One of the most surprising discoveries for me this year was the Museo della Merda, which I learnt about thanks to Felix Burrichter's superb architectural journal *Pin-Up*. It is located on the Castelbosco estate near Piacenza, which belongs to the farmer, researcher, and museologist Gianantonio Locatelli. Locatelli keeps 2,500 cows in his cowsheds there, and every day they provide 30,000 liters of milk for the famous Gran Padano cheese that is produced in that region. As well as the milk the animals also produce dung—100,000 liters a day. For Locatelli this is at least as valuable a raw material as the milk. In state-of-the-art facilities on his farm he extracts methane gas from it, which he then uses to produce energy, as well as manure that he uses to fertilize his fields, and building materials, for instance a kind of brick made from compressed cow dung. The use of animal excrement is a long tradition—from the Egyptians who worshipped the dung beetle, by way of the deliberations of Pliny the Elder in his *Naturalis historia,* to hi-tech uses like lamps based on bio-luminescent bacteria and dung-fuelled heating systems. Finally the raw material has also left its traces on art.

This aspect of the museum is of course what interested me most, for 25 years ago I curated an art exhibition entitled *Cloaca Maxima* at the Museum der Stadtenwässerung, a museum dedicated to sewage in Zurich. Fischli/Weiss, who had tipped me off about the existence of this highly unusual exhibition venue, showed their video about the Zurich sewerage system there, its endless passages only intermittently traversed by a rat; Marcel Duchamp's famous urinal of course played a part, as did Piero Manzoni's project with *Merda d'artista* stored in cans, and Andreas Slominski, who injected fresh urine into a banana every day. It is possible to see some fantastic works in Piacenza too, such as Bernd and Hilla Becher's photographs of gasometers and digestion tanks, and a video by the Swiss artist Daniel Spoerri tracking the path of a steak, from its starting point to its excretion, only shown in reverse. This gives rise to the impression of the perpetual circulation of matter and the great ecological project of recycling that has long played an important role in the agricultural world, but there is still a great deal that we can all learn from it.

Destroyed Memories

September 19, 2015

One of the most exciting aspects of my profession is organizing the first major exhibition for a young artist. In the early 1990s I did this for example with Douglas Gordon and Rirkrit Tiravanija, and in recent years a splendid generation has emerged that has grown up with digital media. Rachel Rose is part of it. Born in 1986, she has already developed an independent artistic voice with her video works. I have been following her development since her student years, and each time we meet she surprises me anew. For her exhibition at the Serpentine Galleries in London we have selected two works (both 2014) I regard as being among her most powerful. One is called *A Minute Ago*, one of the most amazing videos I have seen in recent years, and absolutely riveting. It begins with an apocalyptic hailstorm that sweeps so wildly across a beach that we fear we might immediately be blown away with it. Then music is introduced, a sequence from Pink Floyd's song *Echoes*, which they play in the faded-in empty amphitheater of Pompeii, as if the millennial storm had swept the rest of humankind off the earth. And finally we follow a cine camera through Philip Johnson's famous Glass House, a building that is transcendent and fragile, like our world.

Not only is the effect of the video powerful, but also the way in which Rachel Rose made it: she found the hailstorm on YouTube, the Pink Floyd concert on an old VHS cassette, and finally she herself filmed the Glass House. She set about the second work called *Palisades in Palisades* in quite a similar way. A girl is standing in the Palisades Interstate Park in New York from which the video takes its title, on the bank of the Hudson River, and as she looks at the water, colors and images move across it, like clouds, linking this place with its history—the American revolution and its wars. Rose is concerned with destruction: the destruction of memory in the digital age, but also the destruction of nature and of human beings' relationship with their environment through technology. With the overlaying of partly found, partly self-made video material that really does not fit together and shows events that have nothing to do with one another, she creates a poetic total work of art from color and image that carries the viewer along like a hailstorm.

Fleeing

March 25, 2017

Imagine you are fleeing. You are being pursued by the police, and are carrying the few possessions you still have through the desert, fearing for your life. No, you are quite right, it is barely possible to imagine this traumatic experience. And yet the Mexican director Alejandro G. Iñárritu, who has won several Oscars, has come fairly close to achieving his goal of making it possible to go through that experience of flight in a virtual reality experiment.

Iñárritu became famous with films such as *Babel*, *The Birdman*, and most recently *The Revenant* (2006, 2014, and 2015), in which Leonardo DiCaprio in the role of the trapper Hugh Glass drags himself across the Rocky Mountains, half dead. The camera, controlled by Iñárritu's long-term artistic associate Emmanuel Lubezki, follows him so unrelentingly as he progresses that as a spectator you have the feeling that you yourself are wandering around in the icy cold. But that is nothing compared with their latest work. It is called *Carne y Arena* and had its premiere at this year's Cannes Film Festival. Now it can be seen at the Fondazione Prada in Milan: you take off your shoes and socks, are given a rucksack and a virtual reality headset, and are sent into an area strewn with sand. While you are in it alone, through the headset you suddenly see a lot of people around you who are likewise walking across the sand of the Mexican desert heading for the United States. But suddenly the ear-splitting noise of helicopters approaches, the wind tears through your hair, and in a trice you are surrounded by police pointing pistols at your chest. This experience, lasting just six-and-a-half minutes, is one of the most gripping things virtual reality has ever produced. Here you are really in it, spatially and with every fiber of your being, and you constantly have to make decisions about whether you communicate and if so with whom, and where you are heading. Iñárritu and Lubezki have used virtuality to create something new and distinctive instead of merely exploiting the technology. When you leave the sandy area you are back in another room in which the refugees you have just seen virtually tell the genuine stories of their journeys. This does not make the fate of millions of refugees more comprehensible. But it does make it more tangible.

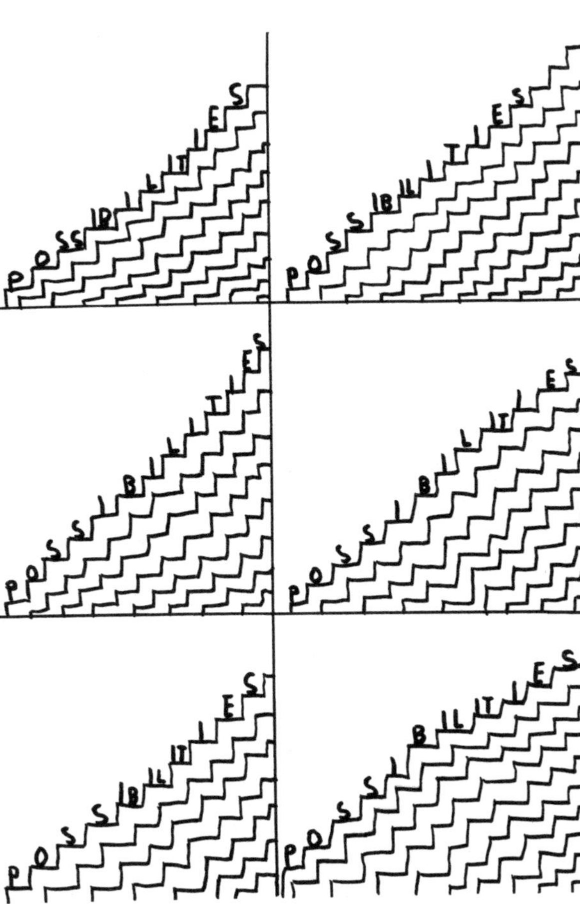

On Hacking

April 16, 2016

A short time ago, together with colleague Amira Gad from the Serpentine Galleries in London, I curated an exhibition with works by Simon Denny (*Hack Space*, K11 Art Foundation). Denny is young, born in Auckland, New Zealand in 1982, and throughout his artistic life he has been pre-occupied by hacking. What is usually understood by "hacking" is when somebody gets into another computer; and depending on the objectives the hacker is pursuing, we regard it as good or bad. In fact the concept in its fundamental meaning in Denny's work tends to be positive: a person who "hacks" something has above all found a solution, a path. "Hacking" in this general sense is then also more related to "cracking" than "breaking in"—you crack a code, a riddle, a problem. A hacker opens up, scrutinizes, and integrates an initially strange, closed system. He is more of an enlightener than a villain. In any case that is how Denny wants his hacking to be understood, even if not everyone sees it that way.

We wanted to show his works in Hong Kong where there is a special situation with regard to hacking, for many people reproach the mother country China with primarily having the fact that it taps into the knowledge of others and hacks into the hard discs of foreign companies to thank for its growing prosperity. Therefore we traveled through the country and asked 11 artists to enhance Denny's exhibition with their works on this theme, and give a context to the concept in their country. The result was more than an update. It gave hacking a completely new philosophical twist. In China they use the all-embracing concept of "shanzhai." This means more or less "emulative creation," a creative principle signifying that no creativity comes out of nowhere. Viewed in this way, the plagiarisms of products for which the country was once famous are just as much "shanzhai" as a work of art whose originator has drawn inspiration from art history. The artist aaajiao demonstrates this by documenting how he himself founded a company; Li Liao "hacked" his way into Foxconn, the mega-enterprise that produces Apple's iPhones, but also mobile devices of its own. They show that not keeping the hacked information for oneself, but making it available to all, is also part of "shanzhai." "Hack and share," that is the message coming out of this exhibition. For without shanzhai, neither the works of Titian nor smartphones would exist.

The Tulip Pyramid

January 28, 2017

If you should be on Instagram, take a look at Alice Rawsthorn's page. She is a critic at the *New York Times* and an indispensable authority for everyone who has anything to do with design. In addition she has one of the best Instagram accounts in existence. Every week she posts on a different subject, and every day puts out a related picture along with an illuminating text. It is impossible to be so well informed that Rawsthorn will ever fail to provide some information you have never come across before.

When I last met her, she recommended a book by a young Chinese designer called Jing He to me. Its title is *Tulip Pyramid* (2016). The tulip pyramid is a one-meter high, multi-storey vase, and tulips can be inserted into it at every level. It was invented by a Dutch porcelain manufacturer in the 17th century, and he gave it an exterior intended to remind people of both ceramics and pagoda architecture from China. Jing He takes the pyramid as the starting-point for asking what Chinese design really is today, given that it was once so unique that 400 years ago it was copied throughout the world.

Today, on the other hand, Jing He writes, China is known first and foremost for copying other people's products and designs. A particularly impressive example of this is the furniture chain Joyme, which imitates everything made by Ikea right down to the assembly instructions in order then to launch its products on the Chinese market at very much lower prices than the Swedish originals. However, over time Joyme has also included its own creations in the program, which are no longer pure copies, but extensions, further developments, adaptations. For Jing He this step indicates an important process: we learn by copying. If you master the copy, you can advance from there. She has also observed the same process on the Chinese market for smartphones: most models look similar to the Apple iPhone. But in contrast to earlier versions, now smartphone designers no longer regard it as so important to design the illusion of an actual iPhone; they are satisfied with the iPhone "look-alikes" being reminiscent of the original—just like an artist who makes a reference in his work to a predecessor he admires. Thus Chinese design, Jing He concludes, is the art of designing a product to make it look like a fake.

Unending

May 23, 2015

When we watch a film we are used to it stopping at some point. Often the tension is actually based on the fact that it does not go on forever, but will come to an end. Of course there are films that last for a very long time, or are told in lots of episodes as a serial. On YouTube we also find videos that are looped, i.e. they always jump back to the beginning at a specific point. But nothing is developed in these videos, they only go on repeating the same thing. What would it be like to see a film that continues forever?

First of all it would be hard for the audience as they would of course have to spend their whole lives in front of the screen, and when they died, only they, but not the film, would have come to an end. But above all the director would inevitably have problems unless he does what Ian Cheng has done. The young artist who lives in New York creates cyber-worlds whose structures he was able to study when he animated Hollywood films and video games for major production companies. The technology, as well as his abilities as a programmer, became ever more refined, and the virtual worlds ever more realistic. They have just one defect: at some point the video game or the film comes to an end. Cheng therefore wrote a computer program that breathed a kind of soul into the virtual characters. Algorithms decide what the avatars will do next. Everything is in constant movement and development—even the way in which the computer humans communicate with one another. For Cheng not only puts living creatures, stones, and trees into his computer world, but signs and symbols as well; the humans have to learn to come to terms with these, slowly at first, until at some point perhaps a language will evolve. Cheng projects his unending story onto two screens, as he is currently doing at the Fondazione Sandretto Re Rebaudengo in Turin. On one we see a landscape panorama with traces of an early civilization that seems threatened with extinction. On the other he zooms onto isolated individuals. So in this live simulation of the history of civilization we can observe at the macro and the micro level how human beings learn to build houses, or simply just to trust one another. Although if you want to know how things work out in the medium term, you need to have a bit of time to spare. Around ten thousand years should be enough for a first impression.

The Great Game

December 14, 2013

The Egyptian artist Wael Shawky has embarked on a rather ambitious experiment. With the aid of huge technical and craft resources he is staging events from the often bloody history of the Middle East as a play, from the momentous dispute about the legitimate succession to the Prophet Mohammed in the 7th century that led to the split into the Shiite and Sunni denominations, to the assassination of President Sadat of Egypt in 1981. The protagonists are often puppets whose activities he documents in epic filmic artworks. Controlled on threads by unseen hands, they murder or, as in the two-part film *Cabaret Crusades* (2010–ongoing), are themselves murdered. It is interesting to see that Shawky recounts the history of the Crusades from the Eastern point of view, which is not very familiar to us Western viewers. But while he enacts history as a puppet show, he is primarily making something different clear: this is only one variation of the staging. For it is us, the people of today, who interpret the past in whatever way we now please.

Shawky, still a young man, has brought navigating between facts and fiction, between theatrical reality and the actuality of countless dead, between play and seriousness, to a point of virtuosity that has led to him being regarded as one of the foremost artists of the present day. Just recently here at the Serpentine Galleries he presented his latest work (*Al Araba Al Madfuna II*), a film in which he features children dressed as adults and with adult voices. They reenact some fairy tales by the Egyptian writer Mohamed Mustagab. They are cruel parables about vengeance and death that the children enact with great seriousness and a frightening matter-of-factness. There are many different, very contradictory interpretations of these films. Their richness is the best proof that Shawky's art is so very much more thoughtful and intelligent than most of what we read and hear about the Middle East from so many leaders of opinion of every persuasion.

To Counter Forgetting

September 12, 2015

In Johannesburg I recently met Santu Mofokeng who photographed street scenes in the townships even as a young man, and has since become not only one of the most important chroniclers of this tension-filled country, but also one of the greatest photographers of the present day. As Mofokeng had lost his voice because of a nervous disorder, we had to communicate in writing. I asked him a question, and he wrote his answers down for me in a book. He told me that the greatest influence on him had been David Goldblatt, the world-renowned photographer who is his senior by a quarter of a century and the mentor of the photography scene in South Africa. Goldblatt encouraged him as he did many others, and inspired him to a form of photography carrying a political message, which in the days of apartheid was not devoid of risk. Mofokeng's pictures are also political, especially his early shots of everyday life in Soweto, and his portraits, as well as the panoramas of the landscapes devastated by mining.

Yet the political element in his images is always also permeated or accompanied by a spiritual dimension. That becomes particularly clear in his most recently implemented project, the series on graves. In it he shows the final resting places of members of South African populations whose burial sites had to give way to new platinum, gold, and silver mines. Right across the country thousands of inhabitants were robbed of their geographical and spiritual homeland by their white rulers, and therefore of their collective memory. The loss of memory is the third aspect that runs through Mofokeng's work. In his series of photographs about dances, advertising hoardings, or the prison island Robben Island, he conducts a campaign against forgetting— the forgetting of black culture and the atrocities of apartheid. He documents South Africa's past not only as a traditional photographer, but also as a conceptual one, for example in his book *The Black Photo Album* (2013). In it he reproduces pictures from the photograph albums of black South African families, accompanied by texts that are derived from interviews with those families, often telling dramatic stories. Currently Mofokeng is working on a series of 18 books of photographs that the highly regarded publishing house Steidl is devoting to the complex themes the artist covers. After their publication if not before, Santu Mofokeng will be assured of a place among the truly great in the history of photography in the 20th and 21st centuries.

Tell Me Your Secret

October 16, 2015

In the 1970s you could repeatedly come across very curious ads in a small art journal published in Amsterdam. A certain Hreinn Friðfinnsson requested readers to entrust him with their secrets. At the time only a few people knew who this Mr. Friðfinnsson was, but because of his advertisement that was circulated in the art world, soon a lot of people got to hear of this Icelandic Conceptual artist. Rumors and surmises did the rounds: that he would get up to the strangest things with these secrets; or that it was really a campaign that was only disguised as art; or indeed that, quite on the contrary, a new art form was in the process of being created in which the work was not only—as is the principle in Conceptual art—an invisible intellectual concept, but also unknown, strictly secret. Thus over the years Friðfinnsson's "Secrets Project" became his most famous work, although—or perhaps precisely because—nobody knew whether it really existed. More than caring about the secrets as such, people were primarily interested in the secret of whether this artwork existed.

Friðfinnsson often plays with memories and perceptions, using them as fluid material. With his poetic works that often have something of the novel about them, he has long since ensured himself a place as an important contemporary artist, even over and above his "Secrets Project." However, 40 years later the artist is lifting the veil. At the Kunstverein in Amsterdam he is showing the "Secrets Project," consisting of the ads and a monochrome painting where the paint conceals the secrets collected. For a long time the artist himself did not know that there would actually be an artwork relating to the secrets. For as he once told me, if he were to exhibit the secrets, then they would no longer be secrets. Immediately he showed his collection, it would have ceased to exist. By exhibiting the fact that he is keeping them hidden, he has found a solution. Of course the other question is whether he actually has anything to hide. Friðfinnsson makes no bones about the fact that not a single person responded to his original advertisements; however, a few years ago he repeated the ad in a magazine with a lot of readers. Some people may have written to him, perhaps even telephoned him. How many of them there were, and what they said, we will certainly never learn.

Extra-Terrestrial

May 10, 2014

When Peter Fischli and David Weiss advised me to visit H. R. Giger's workshop in 1985, he was already world-famous as the man who had designed the visual effects for Ridley Scott's classic science-fiction movie *Alien*, and been awarded an Oscar for it—a rare honor for a Swiss national. And when I recently met Paul Chan at the Schaulager for the opening of his exhibition, he too told me how much he admired Giger—as someone who describes a world as it might look after the Apocalypse, but first and foremost as a stunning graphic artist. This latter aspect may perhaps have been somewhat lost from view because Giger was never "only" an artist; he also created posters and calendars, record sleeves and playing cards, electric guitars, and even video games, which made him into a cult figure in the horror and science-fiction scenes.

We only have to take a look at *Alien Diaries*, two brilliant sketchbooks made while working on the film and published in a beautiful edition last year, or the *Necronomicon* picture books (1985), to be aware of Giger's incredible creative energy. Inspired by the American horror fiction writer H. P. Lovecraft, he created a parallel world consisting of extra-terrestrials, monsters, and the undead, in a style perhaps reminiscent of Alfred Kubin, and certainly of the Surrealism of Salvador Dalí, with whom he was furthermore linked by the fact that both men were unabashed about popularizing art. The discovery of the airbrush technique and his acquaintance with Albert Hofmann who invented LSD and reinforced his interest in psychedelic experiences had a defining influence on him. How strong an impact these experiences had on his plan to tunnel under the whole of Switzerland in 1993 is not known. In any case, Federal President Ogi apparently thanked him very amicably for the suggestion. When I finally visited Giger in his house in Oerlikon with his publisher Patrick Frey a few weeks ago, I stepped into a total work of art full of strange found objects, technoid creatures, and figures of aliens. Unfortunately there is as yet no public access to his house. Even so, it is possible meanwhile to get some idea of Giger's cosmos from his private museum in Gruyère in the canton of Fribourg.

A Work and Teamwork

March 4, 2017

It began with fake news. In a radio program someone had claimed that the painter Albert Oehlen was working on a series of paintings while traveling up and down on a hydraulic lift, on each occasion taking the places he had just arrived at as his subject matter. That was pure invention; but Oehlen found the idea so curious that he called his most recent cycle of works "Elevator Paintings," after that anecdote. He told me this a few weeks ago in New York. For it so happened that we were staying in the same hotel, and for a few days saw one another at breakfast every morning. Of course I already knew him before that: he is one of the most important painters of the present day. Just last year I interviewed him in the context of the Engadin Art Talks, and I once visited him in his studio in Gais in Switzerland, where he has lived for many years. I have a special relationship with Gais because as student I established a Robert Walser museum there; it was in the Hotel Krone, where Walser used often to go for a meal after walking for hours.

When I came to see Oehlen's most recent pictures, I immediately associated them with Walser. Not because some of them were painted in Gais, but because the organic, sinuous lines on these paintings are reminiscent of lifelines and—very much in the spirit of Walser—they are walking across the canvas. That is especially true of the tree pictures, which are generally restricted to black and red. On the aforesaid "Elevator Paintings" too, streaks and tracks form coils, yet every contour is threatened with its own dissolution, and the whole composition is held in a delicate balance between form and formlessness. It is no accident that this description of a picture resembles the way people talk about music. For among Oehlen's many merits is the fact that he has transferred not only compositional principles, but also many of the music world's working methods into the sphere of visual art by often collaborating with other artists or musicians—such as the German techno pioneer Holger Hiller—on a work. Unlike in art, above all in the current rap and hip hop scene, it is completely normal for an artist to abolish the boundaries between individual and collective creative achievement for a single piece, or for several, and to take on board the best singers and musicians in order to obtain the best result.

The Listener

The art world owes just as much to John Berger who died on January 2 as it does to its greatest artists. In Great Britain, nobody who is interested in art does not know and honor this man. For Berger gave access to painting, sculpture, and photography to countless people, even and especially those who came from a supposedly uneducated strata of society. He succeeded in doing this principally through "Ways of Seeing," a series of BBC television programs in which he made the richness of an artwork visible to a public of millions. He showed how it is possible to enjoy art without having to know a great deal about it; that patience is sometimes required, and that you have to "listen" to a picture for a long time before it speaks to you; and that once the conversation between the work and the viewer has begun, an unending, exhilarating dialogue develops—and hence what is commonly described as "art appreciation."

John Berger's unique achievement was first and foremost to listen. He had so much to say because he had absorbed so much in such a concentrated way. All his writings, whether novels, short stories, films, or art criticism, were the product of his talent for immersing himself so much in his opposite number that he himself became that other. I last had the good fortune to meet this impressive man four years ago. It was on the stage at the Serpentine Galleries during a 48-hour Memory Marathon. He read a piece from a short story he was in the process of writing. In it he is sitting in his house in France and sees a report on television about riots in Croydon, a problematic town adjoining London. Houses and shops are on fire, including a furniture store. He remembers walking past that store with his mother when he was an 11-year-old boy. Every week she would take him with her to the supermarket, he would help her carry the shopping, and when they were finished they would go the cinema together. But what on earth was the supermarket called? When the name finally came back to him, it was as if his long deceased mother were suddenly sitting beside him.

Now, after his death, thousands of visitors to museums will have a quite similar experience when they stand in front of a picture and look at it for a long time. If a silent conversation then finally begins, it will be as if John Berger were standing right alongside, and listening in.

The Strolling Artist

March 2, 2013

Around 2008 a rumor came from Brazil that there was an artist who kept covering huge distances on foot. Because in a way I am a pupil of Lucius Burckhardt who invented strollology in his day, I immediately felt curious. The said artist is still quite young, born in 1977, and his name is Paulo Nazareth. He did indeed walk barefoot from Brazil to New York, gathering dust along the way, and at the end of the journey that took weeks he washed his feet in the Hudson River in a quasi-religious act. Currently he is crossing Africa, again on foot. On the way he collects what he finds—nuts, impressions, rubbish—and then arranges all the found objects into installations in a sort of individual mythology, as the great curator Harald Szeemann described it. But these arrangements are only a small part of Nazareth's wide-ranging oeuvre. And they are more by-products of his real major achievement, the strolling performances that in their length, rigor, and physical difficulty have founded a completely new genre in performance art.

Nazareth came to prominence in 2011 with a work he showed at Art Basel in Miami Beach. It is called *Banana Market/Art Market*, and consists of a green VW van laden with bananas, obviously implying a parallel between the market for bananas and the art market. Even though Nazareth has now come to be represented by a gallery and is currently being given his first comprehensive show at the Museu de Arte de São Paulo, he is at least just as interested in taking art to places where there is no art as to places where it exists in (banana-like) quantities. For what really matters to him, so he told me, is the ephemeral, the fleeting, and what lies at the edge where nobody else goes and looks. Nazareth has chosen this walking to out-of-the-way places as his concept. He collects and draws what he encounters on the way, films and photographs it. He weaves these found objects into installations, videos, and his blog, and spins new tales from them. As a thoughtful, active walker he puts a world of his own into the found world.

Old Lady, Youthful Art

May 31, 2014

Shortly before her death on May 6 of this year, 94-year-old Maria Lassnig wrote me a letter she was unable to complete. The fragment ends with the sentences: "In the company of art we don't go to pieces. Without art, we do, and I especially do."

I do not know many people who have lived for art to the same extent as the Austrian graphic artist, painter, and animated filmmaker Maria Lassnig. She really bears comparison only with the American sculptress Louise Bourgeois who died in 2010. They were both among the most significant women artists of the 20th century; not only are we indebted to them for sublime works, but also for their struggle to achieve equal recognition for women artists in an art world dominated until quite recently by men. In Vienna in the 1950s Lassnig inclined toward the *informel*, as postwar abstract painting was designated in Europe, but very soon she turned to her lifelong theme: body awareness pictures. It is apparent in them why art had such existential significance for her: she regarded body and image as an inseparable couple. The transcendence of her art always begins with the body, and in the body images she develops an intensity that leads her to a higher, universal stage of a condensed self. This attitude also makes her a precursor of Viennese Actionism, which regarded the artist's own body as his or her only material.

The recognition accorded to her came late. It is only this year that her first major museum exhibition is being held at MoMA PS1 in New York, where she lived for over ten years. I got to know Maria Lassnig in 1993 in Vienna during preparations for the group exhibition *The Broken Mirror* I curated with Kasper König, and I was immediately overwhelmed by how vital her pictures appeared among the works of younger artists. I also studied her writings and drawings that played such a major role in her work, because she constantly developed and altered her theme in them. "A drawing," she once said to me, "makes it possible to recognize a question over and over again in a new light." The bodies in her pictures became older, but the artist Maria Lassnig remained youthful even at a great age.

Bring Down the Curtain!

January 31, 2015

Somewhere in his mammoth book *The Man Without Qualities* (1930–1932) Robert Musil wrote that art often turns up where it is least expected— and then also has a quite special effect. This idea of showing art in places where it is not expected has interested me from my earliest beginnings when I put on exhibitions in my kitchen, in a hotel, or in a restaurant. In the 1990s this approach continued to be developed at institutional level too, and art suddenly appeared not only in public squares, but also on advertising hoardings, and even on planes. The "museum in progress" in Vienna is a survivor from those days; it is not in fact a museum in the true meaning of the word, but a place that enables art. One of its projects consists of commissioning a different artist each year to design the fire curtain at the Vienna State Opera. The location is ideal for an artwork, for the audience—hundreds of thousands of people in a year—does indeed spend a relatively long time in front of the concealed stage before the beginning of the performance and during the intervals. Since 1998 such celebrated artists as Richard Hamilton, Maria Lassnig, Rosemarie Trockel, Jeff Koons, and David Hockney have displayed their designs on the huge picture surface framed by the proscenium arch (see mip.at). This year it is the legendary video and performance artist Joan Jonas whose work is currently also on view at the Hangar Bicocca in Milan, and will be from May—as the representative of the United States in the American pavilion—at the Venice Biennale.

Jonas is an ideal piece of casting for the opera. She was born in 1936 and has lived in New York ever since, where her works have focused on theater since the 1960s. In many of her performances she involves actors, dancers, and props, often the audience as well. Since the end of the 1990s she has created a series of works, *My New Theater*, consisting of propped-up plywood boxes. If you look into them, you see videos of performances, as in a virtual mini-theater. For Vienna Jonas has prepared a drawing inspired by Celtic rituals, which for their part are precursors to theater productions. At first it looks very simple, based on a kind of labyrinth, but the more profoundly you become immersed in it, the more confusing the interplay between the micro and the macro level of the lines becomes,

until you finally get completely lost in the labyrinth—as in a thrilling opera.

On Art that Doesn't Tip Over

March 16, 2013

The good thing about art in public space is that it is also seen by people who do not go to museums. On the other hand, many of these works that do not always have a lot to set against the triviality of shopping streets and new estates come time and time again from the same set of artists who virtually form a professional group of their own. It generally becomes interesting only when truly great artists like the Swiss duo Peter Fischli & David Weiss occasionally abandon the gallery and take their art outside. Anyone who has ever traveled from Zurich Airport into the city by train has probably seen their superb mural *How To Work Better* (1991)—ten rules on optimizing work which they saw in a Thai factory, photographed, and transplanted in huge letters on to an office building in Oerlikon.

Their most recent public work *Rock on Top of Another Rock* is also a kind of transplant. It was conceived in 2009, so before David Weiss' death last year, and has now been implemented. They brought two one-meter high boulders from

Wales to Kensington Gardens in London, and placed them on top of one another in such a way that you think the top rock might crash down if given only a gentle push. The construction appears reckless and extremely precarious, but the rocks of course weigh tons and cannot be moved as much as a millimeter by a human hand. We unveiled the work today in front of the Serpentine Galleries (which is in the middle of the park), and seeing it there I was forcibly reminded of Fischli/Weiss' *Equilibres/ Quiet Afternoon* series I had seen in their studio in 1985 when I was still at school. Like the rocks, the series consists of photographs of everyday objects stacked onto and into one another until they are on the verge of tipping over or collapsing. The impression made on me then in the studio was so powerful that I decided to dedicate myself to art for the rest of my life. Twenty-eight years have passed since then, but the impact made by the two great Swiss artists has remained. I stood in the park for the whole afternoon and evening and looked. Not a single one of the hundreds of joggers and walkers who came past failed to stop, laugh, shudder, or marvel.

Richter and Pärt

August 22, 2015

Linking the arts with one another is one of the concerns closest to my heart. Such links can be produced by means of conferences, books in which the widest variety of authors are involved, exhibitions of course, but also by bringing together people who are among the most out-standing exponents of their subject. I once had a conversation about this with Alex Poots, the director of the Manchester International Festival (2005–2015), and we undertook to bring about such a cooperation at the highest level. After many years of persuasion, this has now been successfully achieved with two of the greatest living artists, the painter Gerhard Richter whom I know very well, and the composer Arvo Pärt with whom Poots has collaborated for many years. Both Richter and Pärt have long appreciated one another's work. Richter told me many years ago that he often listened to works by Pärt. He has already collaborated with musicians before—he has designed a concert poster for the composer Glenn Branca and a record cover for the band Sonic Youth, made a book with the minimal music pioneer Steve Reich, and created works in homage to Johann Sebastian Bach and John Cage.

Both Richter and Pärt were born in the 1930s, grew up under Communist regimes—one in the former GDR, the other in Estonia, at that time a Soviet republic—and both had likewise experienced World War II. They drew on this shared biographical heritage when Richter embarked on the abstract cycle *Birkenau*—four paintings he created after photographs of a detainee at the Auschwitz-Birkenau concentration camp. But the two men are also linked by their artistic practice that on the one hand leaves room for chance, and on the other often verges on minimalism. A series of gray pictures on show last year at the Richter exhibition at the Fondation Beyeler were created in this spirit. Pärt composed a piece entitled *Drei Hirtenkinder aus Fátima*, sung a cappella by a choir to accompany both groups of works. The effect of this coproduction that was first performed this year in Manchester was overwhelming. Many visitors who were standing among the singers in the gallery wept. In the few minutes when these beautiful voices rang out in front of Richter's pictures, we felt as if the whole world were dissolving.

Sound Without Place

February 1, 2014

How is it possible that there really is no museum for sound? We have museums for everything—for art, for literature, for history, for technology, even one for curried sausage. But not for sound. By this I do not mean pop music, or classical music either, which can be heard in the appropriate concert halls and concert houses. I mean the music that requires a different architectural framework in order to be experienced properly. New Music falls into this category: minimalist or electronic music by composers such as Karlheinz Stockhausen, Steve Reich, or Brian Eno, who in their very individual ways have developed new technologies, sounds, and types of performance that do not fit into any established framework. Iannis Xenakis gave me the idea of a sound museum. I have interviewed him and many other exponents of experimental music in the past and have now published these interviews as a book with JRP|Ringier. They all had and have the problem of finding a location for their music. But Xenakis has tried to find a solution.

He was predestined to do this. Born in 1922, he first studied engineering in Athens, then went to Paris where he worked with and for Le Corbusier, but he was already taking lessons in composition on the side because he saw a connection between the construction of space and of sound. In 1951 he became a pupil of Olivier Messiaen, one of the foremost composers of the 20th century, and soon Xenakis himself was among them too. But as he did not want to think of music without thinking of the space it sounds in, he developed "polytopes" (literally, many places): spaces that alter with sound, especially through changing light effects. The audience in them was not static either. Sometimes they walked around, as in 1971 in the ruinous landscape of Persepolis that Xenakis transformed into an experimental total work of art with laser flashes and loud-speakers; sometimes they lay down, sometimes they leant on metal pipes, as in the Roman baths of the Musée de Cluny in Paris. Unfortunately however, these were all only temporary installations. We are still waiting for a permanent home for experimental sounds today.

Zaha Hadid

April 9, 2016

When I first visited Zaha Hadid in her studio at the end of the 1990s, I went not only because of her architecture, but also to get to know Hadid as an artist. She was a fervent admirer of Russian Constructivism and created superb paintings that were influenced by Malevich, Tatlin, and Rodchenko. A London black cab fetched me from the airport and took me to Hadid's studio, at that time still quite a small one, in which an atmosphere of emergence could be sensed, like that which must have also prevailed among the Russian avant-gardists of the 1920s. Just three months later when we were already working together on a project for the park of the Villa Medici in Rome, I visited her again. I was a little surprised when I realized that the same taxi driver was collecting me. When he was at the wheel on a third occasion too, only a short while later, and I commented on this coincidence to him in some perplexity, he enlightened me, explaining it was one of his boss Hadid's many unconventional whims to have bought herself a taxi that drove only herself and her visitors.

Zaha Hadid was so far removed from all artistic and architectural standards and conventions that it took a long time for her to gain the recognition that was her due, and ultimately become a celebrity who built some of most iconic buildings of the 21st century in Vienna, Abu Dhabi, London, and Guangzhou. Born in Baghdad in 1950, for her it was especially important that she should erect buildings in the Arab world. For among the many as yet undiscovered facets of Hadid are her calligraphies, inspired by Arabic characters: in their serpentine forms we can recognize the sweep of her architectonic designs. The first building she implemented in London, where she had been living for decades, was a pavilion for the Serpentine Galleries in 2000, with which the Galleries founded the tradition of having a pavilion built in Kensington Gardens, designed by a different architect every year. Hadid's design radiated the whole lightness and weightlessness of her buildings, which seem more to hover than to weigh down on the ground. She put all her energy, she once told me, into the attempt to suspend the laws of nature, gravitation, and death. I am infinitely sad at the loss of this visionary architect, artist, and friend.

Go and Make Me a Coffee!

September 15, 2012

It is already astonishing to realize that the buildings we live in were almost exclusively designed by men. But it is almost more astonishing still that Lina Bo Bardi, one of the first female architects to have an international influence on many young architects still today, is only now coming to the attention of a wider public. The Venice Architecture Biennale curated by Kazuyo Sejima devoted itself to her two years ago, and an exhibition curated by Noemi Blager has just started at the British Council Gallery in London. Bo Bardi was born in 1914; in the 1940s she worked in Milan before migrating to Brazil where she designed some of the most remarkable buildings in Latin America. One of them is the Glass House, which floats on stilts in dense woodland on a hill above São Paulo, where she lived with her husband, the museum director Pietro Bardi.

Today the house is the headquarters of the Bardi Foundation, and in recent years it has not been accessible to the public. I wanted to change that. So I initiated a house exhibition that is dedicated to both the individual and the building. Gilbert & George will sit by the hearth as living sculptures, Cinthia Marcelle has an orchestra rehearsing a soundtrack special to the house based on Bardi's record collection, and Cildo Meireles is producing an installation in which Pietro Bardi's voice rings out and the smell of coffee fills the air. For however perfect the harmony of light and geometry of the house may be, that between its occupants was not always quite so flawless—political discussions used to end with him telling her: Fammi un caffè, go and make me a coffee!

I like these small exhibitions in private houses, and have already organized ones along similar lines in García Lorca's house in Granada, and Nietzsche's house in Sils Maria. They are a counter-weight to the ever-larger international exhibitions, and they prompt artists to create small-scale works that they would perhaps not make for an outsize show. Unlike a museum, a house has human dimensions. And those dimensions are valid for both the architecture and the art.

The Pyramids of Ivry-sur-Seine

August 5, 2017

The Grenfell Tower fire in North Kensington in London where at least 80 people lost their lives profoundly shocked me. Not just because I live in London, but also because I deal with architecture and architects on a daily basis. The fact that such a catastrophe could happen as a result of the sheer neglect of regulations and a failure of state supervision at a time of hi-tech materials and an unparalleled wealth of architectonic ideas and resources is really incredible.

But the disaster has prompted me to take a closer interest in the history of social housing, looking for architectural solutions that are more sensitive and less catastrophe-prone that the tower block in London. The crucial tip came from the architectural critic Niklas Maak, who advised me to go to Paris and meet the architect Renée Gailhoustet. I duly did so, and in fact met her in a house she herself designed, in which she still lives today: a structure of greenery-covered terraces piled beside and above one another to form a garden pyramid. Gailhoustet, an impressive woman who is now 87 years old, and one of the very few notable female architects of her generation (with male dominance unfortunately having changed very little even today), at the time came to architecture by way of politics. As a fervent Communist she wanted equal living conditions for everyone, but saw that she would get closest to that goal if she designed those living conditions herself. Inspired on the one hand by the giant "living machines" of the Swiss-French architect Le Corbusier, on the other sustained by the conviction that every resident of a house needs a space that s/he can shape individually, she invented her iconic terraced housing. Initially as the chief planning officer for Ivry-sur-Seine, a suburb of Paris, and then in many other localities in France, in the 1960s and 1970s, often working in collaboration with Jean Renaudie, she designed convoluted pyramids that give each dwelling a different ground plan, created private and communal gardens, flooded the residential houses with light, and turned commerce, housing, and industry into a transparent social mix. Hers are some of the most humane forms of large-scale buildings I have ever seen.

The Architect
of the Invisible

November 28, 2015

There are architects who build houses. And there are architects for whom it is not just about a specific building, but also about the question of what it actually means to build. Philippe Rahm is one of the latter. In 2002 he attracted great attention with his design for the Swiss Pavilion at the Venice Architecture Biennale. Since then he has emerged as a theoretician, especially in his book *Architecture météorologique* (2009); the theories proposed in it are once again currently dominating architectural debate in France. By meteorological architecture Rahm means a planning and design approach that comprises not only the traditional elements such as walls, roofs, and windows, but also invisible things such as temperature, dryness and damp, smell, and the temperature impact of light. Against the background of the dramatic climatic changes that are being discussed at the Global Climate Change Conference in Paris, his ideas should fall on fertile ground: the building industry is indirectly responsible for 50% of the greenhouse gases emitted worldwide, as a particularly large quantity of fossil fuels is burnt to heat and cool badly designed buildings, according to him. However, rather than making the obvious demand for more energy-sustainable building, the case he makes is decidedly more original: he does not want to build to *counter* global warming, humidification, and ever more powerful storms, but to go *with* them. Vapor, wind, and light are to be the building blocks of a new architecture.

In this Rahm reminds us of the vision of the British architect Cedric Price who once said that the architecture of the 21st century would have to consist of pumping oxygen into the world's great cities. We also think of the words of the American anthropologist Margaret Mead. As far back as the 1940s she criticized European architecture and art as being too strongly focused on visual stimuli, contrasting them with the ritual spaces of Balinese culture; or indeed the church architecture of the Middle Ages which took into consideration smells such as incense, acoustics, and the sensation of the physical closeness of many people. Rahm also advocates the kind of architecture that addresses all the senses and embraces all elements of nature, and it is to be hoped that he will be heard loud and clear beyond the confines of the French-speaking world.

My Aladdin Moment

February 11, 2017

From time to time I would go to a fashion show. This January, for example, I was at London Fashion Week Men's. I always find fashion interesting if it is wearable as well. Not every item has to be capable of being worn every day, especially not those on the catwalk, but designers who think only experimentally, and not in the least practically, just do not particularly interest me. Last year, again in London where a great deal is going on in the fashion world, I made an incredible discovery: Grace Wales Bonner, who has come to be regarded as one of the most promising designers of the present day, showed designs there that were made neither only for women nor only for men. Their cut looks neither unambiguously European, nor African, nor Asian, rather the clothes have something of everything, and are androgynous without being distant, elegant without being minimalist. I certainly would not have expected such a fashion wake-up call to be repeated so soon.

But then I saw Craig Green's clothes. He is master of both—the visionary and the pragmatic. The latter quality is manifested in the block-cut hoodie sweaters, denim jackets, and wide-legged trousers he enhances with small but effective details such as drawstrings. There are many avowed fans of this daywear fashion for men—available moreover at affordable prices; and interestingly enough those fans include many women too. Rihanna for example wears Green's clothes both on and off stage. But it is Green's visionary designs that have blown my mind. Every designer needs these. Not to sell in the shop, but to tell us what he or she stands for. They are an expression not only of the craft skill involved in design, but also of the designer's idealistic and artistic creative strength. It is his drapes in particular that attest to this; they look as if they consist of strips of carpet. They appear tremendously solid, like a protective layer shielding the wearer and keeping them on the ground. On the other hand they make us think of a magic carpet. Green himself has spoken of his "Aladdin moment" when he created them. This very visible contrast, of living room and miracle cure, of feet-on-the-ground and hovering, is an oxymoron, of the kind that often characterizes great art.

Meanwhile, since the photo shoot wearing the Green design that I allowed myself to be talked into by *Das Magazin*, I can say that the Aladdin drapes not only look tremendous (perhaps even a bit more so on other models than me), but are also very comfortable to wear. Green is still very young, even for that field of activity. He was born in North London in 1986, and until recently lived there with his mother; and as the well-known fashion blogger and journalist Charlie Porter wrote in the *Financial Times*, has remained a modest person of integrity in every other respect. I hope that he sustains this oxymoron: to remain modest and brilliant.

New Fashion

July 11, 2015

Ten minutes before I started writing this column, I was still sitting with Grace Wales Bonner and had the strong feeling that I was speaking with a woman who could one day be among the great fashion designers of the 21st century. The things she said, the designs she showed me, and the attention she has aroused in such a short time remind me of another designer. In the 1980s I had a conversation with the Swiss costume designer Madlaina Peer, who told me about a little fashion boutique in Rome, saying I simply had to visit the shop and its owner. I drove there, and was completely bowled over by the fashion of a certain Miuccia Prada.

Just as we then heard people speaking about Prada, today the talk everywhere is about Wales Bonner, not only in the fashion world, but also in the art world, in publishing, and among musicians. On the one hand this has to do with her fashion shows. They are not simply catwalks, but staged total works of art with tremendous music, models the like of whom are otherwise barely seen on the runway, and are accompanied by brilliantly designed artist's books. But above all there is her fashion. Describing her as "androgynous" does not quite hit the mark. Wales Bonner does not make styles for men with feminine characteristics, or for women with masculine ones. Her designs, and she touches a nerve with them, seem not to be in the least interested in the distinction that divides the traditional fashion world into menswear and women's wear. Her designs can be worn by each and every one. Nor does she participate in the everlasting hunt, as she told me, for the always identical and almost always white international top models, but selects the most marvelous models from Africa and throughout the world that nobody else comes up with.

It is crazy that we still go on seeing almost solely white people on the catwalk. In portrait galleries it is unfortunately a similar story. Wales Bonner also reminds me all the more of Lynette Yiadom-Boakye, whose work we are currently showing at the Serpentine Galleries: she portrays exclusively black people. Wales Bonner explicitly invokes her as an inspiration. If, as I hope, she finds the recognition she deserves worldwide, not only fashion, but models too, could finally become a bit more diverse.

MEETING TO DECIDE THE FUTURE

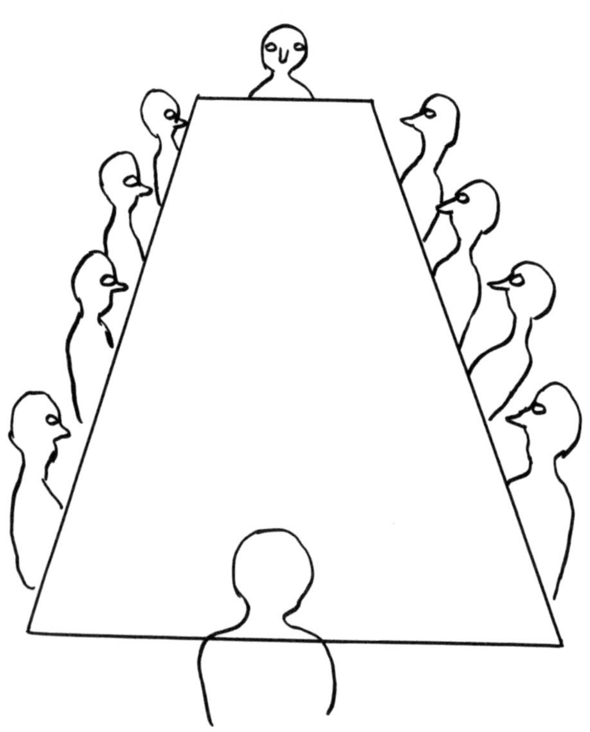

Today
Tomorrow
Time

About Tomorrow

October 1, 2016

In September, the "Shanghai Project" got under way, a kind of festival of ideas about the world in a hundred years' time. The preparation for this event that will continue into the coming year was not all that simple, for I had to recognize that astonishingly few people have thought about how the 22nd century should be imagined. I was not only surprised, but also a little concerned to find such a scarcity of prophecies— as if hardly anybody believed that the 22nd century would happen at all. Until the new book by Yuval Noah Harari came out, mapping out the future so clear-sightedly and plausibly that we tend to feel we are reading a factual report rather than a supposition. The historian who earned his doctorate at Oxford teaches the fine subject of world history at the Hebrew University of Jerusalem. His interest always focuses on the larger whole, the connections between history and biology, the question of fairness in all civilizations, and whether happiness accompanies human beings on their evolutionary path. Many of these questions are dealt with in Harari's bestseller, *A Brief History of Humankind*, which has been translated into nearly 30 languages, and accessed countless times in the form of a free online course.

What now follows is the continuation, *A Brief History of Tomorrow*, published this year by Harvill Secker. The scenario oscillates between enthusiasm and disenchantment. Harari enthusiastically conjures up a world in which intelligent machines, programmed by human beings, can accomplish practically everything, and assume a god-like role. On the other hand the consequences for human beings themselves are sobering: they become useless. Not in the moral sense of course, but economically: since the machines and cyborgs can do everything, there is no longer anything left for human beings to do. They take refuge in virtual realities, but at the same time in clear moments ask themselves the question: In what does their meaning consist? Interestingly enough, Harari finds an existential reason for the human being in an area that no science-fiction author has yet considered: in art. For art is the only thing that machines cannot produce, nor they can experience it.

A Disc for E.T.

July 9, 2016

The signs and symbols on the Golden Record are hard even for earth-dwellers to decipher—to extra-terrestrials they might well remain an eternal riddle. Always supposing extra-terrestrials exist, how would we want to be perceived by them? Nasa considered this question before it sent the Voyager 1 and 2 space probes into outer space in 1977. By now they have both left our solar system and are rushing through space toward an unknown destination at 61,000 kilometers an hour. On board, both of them are transporting a Golden Record, a flat, circular analog disc made of gilded copper. At the time, a team led by the astrophysicist and television presenter Carl Sagan stored 115 images on each disc, as well as voice recordings, sounds, and pieces of music. Sagan thought that these would characterize the world in general, and for extra-terrestrials in particular. They include, among other things, a photograph of a tree in Winterthur, the smacking sound of a kiss on the cheek, and the fifth movement of Beethoven's String Quartet No. 13 in B-flat major.

Twenty-five years after this self-description of the world had left the earth's atmosphere, the British artist and director Steve McQueen subjected it to a critical test. In an exhibition at the musée d'Art moderne de la Ville de Paris he projected the images on the disc onto a screen, and backed the slideshow with incomprehensible babble. He thereby made it clear on the one hand that an extra-terrestrial, should they be in a position to play the record at all, would be unable in looking at the pictures to make any sense of them; at the same time he focused our attention on Nasa's selection, which was transmitting the image of a world where there is no poverty, no wars, no religions, no homosexuals, and no people with dark skins.

What self-image would be propelled into the universe today? The publicist Jefferson Hack and I visited Nasa with this question in mid-May, taking a few friends along with us, including the music producer Pharrell Williams, the writer Ben Lerner, and the artist Rachel Rose. Together we want to compile a new, more up-to-date and truly global Golden Record. However, we would then place it not onto an analog support with its pathetically small storage space, but in the form of a programmed DNA capsule. These can be dispatched directly into outer space by the dozen and indestructibly, and convey a more realistic image of our world—for whoever out there may then want to look at it.

THIS   IS   THE   TREE   THAT
I   FELL   FROM

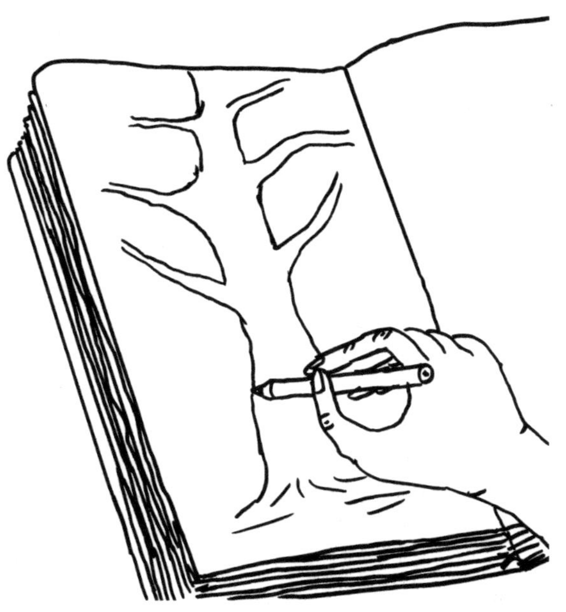

Everything Is Transformed

November 7, 2015

Two thousand years ago, the Roman poet Ovid wrote *Metamorphoses*, in which animals turn into gods, gods into rivers, and human beings into trees. The theme of eternal transformation is as old as the world, but in recent times it has taken on new relevance. It is in the air. So we decided to devote this year's edition of the annual Serpentine Galleries "marathon," the 10th over-all, to transformation. Over a 24-hour period, with no interval, from Saturday morning until Sunday lunchtime, artists, academics, and prac-titioners debated virtually every facet of the topic: Alejandro Jodorowsky, the playwright, reader of tarot cards, and scholar of compara-tive religion, spoke about the forgotten trans-formative science of alchemy, and about cyborgs, i.e. machines that turn into human beings, or human beings who turn into machines. Juliet Jacques also dealt with physical transformation, more specifically the modern pharmacology that makes it possible to switch from one sex to the other. It is not only bodies that change, society, culture, and politics, as well as institutions, the digital world, design, fashion, and literature do too, as the Congolese writer Patrick Mudekereza explained. Our identities are transformed too. An example of this was provided by Gilbert & George, the two artists who discarded their identities in 1968 and have since existed only as a duo.

Finally I was transformed too. At the marathon I had myself metamorphosed by professional make-up artists into the dramatist Heiner Müller who died in 1995, stylistically correct with horn-rimmed glasses and a cigar. The artist Dominique Gonzalez-Foerster, whose idea it was, took on the part of the choreographer Pina Bausch, and for a time we conducted a conversation as Müller and Bausch. When I asked her about an unrealized project, the pretend Bausch answered that she had never involved the public—whereupon she spontaneously invited a few of the audience to the stage and rehearsed a short item with them. The marathon does not claim to deal with a topic exhaustively. In the end it is only the participants who are exhausted—they have not closed their eyes all night; it is a question of circling round a topic, picking up new ideas, getting inspiration; of a spark flying at some point that sets us alight—and transforms us.

Novelties from the Future

Adrian Hon is head of a firm that programs computer games, among them the popular hit *Zombies, Run!* Before that he was a neuroscientist at Cambridge and Oxford, then worked as a science journalist, and as an adviser for a Mars simulation in the Utah desert, and for the British Museum in London. Five years ago its Director Neil MacGregor had the idea of expounding the history of the world based on 100 objects from the museum's collections. Hon was so taken by this that he adapted the concept for a project of his own, in which he bundled together his knowledge from his earlier careers: game-playing, thinking, writing, and simulating. Thus the book *A History of the Future in 100 Objects* came into being in 2013.

In the foreword, a fictitious historian—writing in the year 2082—explains that the time has now come to look back over the 21st century. He wants to record for posterity those developments that particularly changed society, and he immediately names two of the most important:

the massive interconnection of people on the one hand, and their physical and intellectual disintegration on the other. Serving to bring society together are technological innovations like Babel, a program that overcomes linguistic boundaries, Silent Messaging, a kind of texting that requires people neither to write nor to speak aloud, or the Brain Bubble, a virtual super-cloud with which the brain of each individual is linked. With the super-brain, if not before, the threshold into science fiction is crossed because technology and the body are here intertwined. Yet the connection of body and mind is still intact. That changes, according to the historian of 2082 alias Adrian Hon, with the triumph of a religious movement. Because the majority of the population is unemployed as a result of automation, this movement advocates the taking of psychotropic drugs that are better than computer games or conventional drugs at enduringly diverting the consciousness from the meaninglessness of existence, and putting it on the path of the Redeemer.

Much about the book is reminiscent of the scenarios of Aldous Huxley or Stanislaw Lem; but Hon tends to provide fragments rather than a coherent picture, and he doesn't describe the situation negatively. On the contrary, the zest with which he tells a story about each of the 100 objects, about "euphoric gastronomy," or a "cure for hatred," rather make us hope that things will not turn out so badly.

About the Collapse
of Clouds

October 19, 2013

Clouds are interesting phenomena. They are so fleeting and insubstantial that we can fly through them in a plane. On the other hand, from time to time downpours pelt down from them that leave whole stretches of countryside under water. The French art historian Hubert Damisch has described this hybrid state of cloud very vividly: it is of course an essential, unmissable component of landscape, but it is almost impossible to record following the rules of linear perspective, and for that reason the art theorists of the Renaissance advised painters against attempting to depict it. The writer Hans Magnus Enzensberger discovered an interesting parallel to a related species, the data cloud, in this cloud paradox: like rain clouds, the data cloud too is a store with no limits or location, and no fixed form, but on the other hand it contains within it the hard data and numbers, retrievable from anywhere via the Internet, which keep stock exchanges, businesses, correspondence, basically the entire world, running.

However, there is one difference: the data cloud could collapse. This could happen if there were a power cut in some of the server and data centers that are scattered across the world. Admittedly this scenario is extremely unlikely, but it makes it clear how closely data consumption and energy consumption are linked. According to a study dated 2011, the Internet's use of electricity corresponded to the output of 30 nuclear power stations. Already today American data centers use up more power than the country's car industry, and for 2015 it is forecast that the needs of the European data centers on their own will correspond to that of eight million households—and that is without counting the energy consumption of PCs, laptops, tablets and smartphones. Perhaps part of the solution to this problem lies in a new kind of data center. In Portugal the architect João Luís Carrilho da Graça has just designed a storage space that in spite of the Portuguese sun, largely cools the processors that get hot as they run without air conditioning, consumes a minimum amount of energy, and itself produces the little it does need via a solar system. Of course that only works in latitudes where there are not so many clouds.

Threatening Drones

April 18, 2015

Everyone is talking about drones. At the same time, we can generally neither see them nor hear them when they are circling above us. The drones themselves, on the other hand, can see us very well: they are photographing and filming us.

Of course that circumstance has not escaped the attention of artists, in particular the British artist James Bridle, who has created a veritable drone art. To show how present the unmanned flying objects are in air space, he used white lines to draw the shadows of drones on streets and squares in London, Istanbul, Washington DC, and São Paulo. Passersby were greatly astonished, for hardly a single one of them had any concept of how enormous the mostly military surveillance drones are, ones that can take clearly defined images from very high up in the air. Adapting a famous statement by Paul Klee, it could be said in Bridle's case that he makes the invisible visible. He shows not only the planes' shadows, but their shadow sites too. On his Dronestagram tumblr he provides aerial pictures of strategic targets destroyed by the military and secret services using drone attacks.

Drones were originally developed for military purposes, but quickly came to be recommended for civilian uses too. They became commercially available a long time ago; farmers check their crops with drones, mountain rescue teams look for missing people with their aid, and the mail order company Amazon has already announced that in future they will dispatch parcels to remoter areas by means of drones. With so much traffic in the air, we have to think not only about new priority rules, but also about some kind of drone driving license. Mind you, in Switzerland there is a plan to do this, and in Italy a regulation of this kind already came into force last year. Genoa University, together with the Alpine Club and Civil Defence, has therefore set up the first university drone course at its campus in Savona. As with a car driving license, there is a theoretical part and a practical part that have to be learnt and passed; among the 14 participants, as well as engineering and robotics students, there are even a few members of an artillery regiment. Already art and a driver's license are associated with the unmanned flying object, so what is still missing is the corresponding science. Thirty years ago the Swiss national Lucius Burckhardt founded the science of walking, known as strollology. Now we are all waiting for dronology.

The Big Bubble

November 14, 2015

Many people think that in my work everything is a matter of speed because I travel a lot and speak so fast. But really the opposite is the case: I work on many projects over a period of decades. One of these is 89plus, a constantly growing network of young artists who were born in (or after) 1989, when the British computer scientist Tim Berners-Lee invented the Internet. At first he called the system "Enquire," i.e. he saw it as a means of open and unrestricted research, which the Internet did indeed become after a while. But then along came algorithms. Large Internet companies like Google and Facebook began no longer to offer open information as in a bazaar, but only a selection of items. The companies analyze when, how often, and on which sites a user calls up which information particularly frequently, and filter an individual profile of interests from that analysis. As a user of search engines one is then supplied only with the information—and of course the advertising too—which interests one most, according to the algorithms. As a result of this selection we are therefore isolated in our own bubble, because things that do not appear appropriate are simply not shown any more. This phenomenon of intellectual isolation was called the "filter bubble" by Eli Pariser in his book of the same name.

The filter bubble is at the center of the most recent 89plus exhibition that is currently on view at the Westbau in Zurich. The impetus comes from the young artists themselves. For not only have my co-curator Simon Castets and I been visiting them for years all around the globe in their studios, we have also been reading the papers they send in on the topics that currently concern them. The bubble is one of their major preoccupations. The works of the 40 or so artists are a piece of research, and all put together are an attempt to translate that research into an exhibition format. In her painting, Louisa Gagliardi reflects how the big bubble surrounds us as we sit glued to our monitors; the Russian Valia Fetisov has programmed a paranoia app that gives us the feeling of constantly being tracked by someone, and Max Hawkins sends visitors out of the exhibition and into the city via a chance-generating algorithm. Out there we once again encounter people who are staring at their screens.

The Beginning and the End

How do I start? Everyone who does or makes anything is faced with that question. Which screw do I start with to assemble the shelf, how do I begin the email, how do I begin this column? The bigger the task, the harder the beginning. So how does one begin a book? Not long ago I met the British author Adam Thirlwell who has just published his third novel *Lurid & Cute*. I asked him whether he had had a plan before he started writing. He thought he had had only a very vague idea and had struggled with a leitmotif that runs through the story line. But then he went over to simply leaving the story line out. To be sure there is still an outline plot: a man wakes up in bed beside someone he does not know, and in what follows he tries to justify the infidelity to himself and to conceal it from his wife. But this unfortunate original situation then actually leads not to a series of events one after the other, but rather to a concert of internal voices within the protagonist which express themselves at times moralistically, at times pragmatically, at times sarcastically, with regard to his situation.

There are always two motivations, Thirlwell said, that lead him to write something: a scenic situation like that of the man in the bed, and a philosophical one. In this case the philosophical question had been the more important one for him, namely, whether and how one can actually make a confession. For while the equivocal hero confesses to many of his misdemeanors, there are competing voices speaking out of him. Sometimes he downplays, sometimes he dramatizes, sometimes he lies, until neither he himself nor the reader really knows any longer whether it is actually one and the same person speaking. The English sometimes becomes halting and wrong, then suddenly the person speaks Russian, Spanish, German, until the individuality of the speaker seems to disintegrate in the tangle of voices. It could be said that the confession is there, but we do not know who the person confessing is. Entire passages consist of sentences that writers such as Proust or Kafka have put in the mouths of their heroes. This disintegration of the self and copying from other sources make the book into a kind of parable about the Internet age as well. For like Thirlwell's hero, the virtual world too is a hybrid, many-voiced construct without a subject, without an end, and therefore also without a beginning.

Index of Names

89plus (36, 190, 191)
aaajiao (125)
Abovitz, Rony (80)
Adler, Karl-Heinz (96, 97)
Adnan, Etel (13, 85, 86, 87, 88)
Af Klint, Hilma (103)
agnès b. (85)
Aitken, Doug (24)
al-Khal, Yusuf (88)
Bach, Johann Sebastian (155)
Ball, Hugo (104)
Balzac, Honoré de (10, 43)
Banzi, Massimo (76, 77)
Baumann, Daniel (95)
Bausch, Pina (181)
Bardi, Lina Bo (160, 161)
Bardi, Pietro (160, 161)
Becher, Bernd and Hilla (118)
Bechtler, Cristina (95)
Van Beethoven, Ludwig (176)
Berger, John (142, 144)
Berners-Lee, Tim (31, 190)
Beuys, Joseph (36, 82)
Beyoncé (106, 107)
Biesenbach, Klaus (24)
Bitelli, Josh (28)
Blager, Noemi (160)
Bode, Sigmund (93)
Boetti, Alighiero (94)
Boltanski, Christian (12)
Boullée, Étienne-Louis (15)
Bourgeois, Louise (14, 30, 147)
Branca, Glenn (154)
Brand, Stewart (115)
Bridle, James (187)
Brockman, John (16, 18)
Bruguera, Tania (83)
Buonarroti, Michelangelo (90)
Burckhardt, Lucius (145, 189)
Burrichter, Felix (117)

Byatt, A.S. (114)
Byars, James Lee (18)
Cage, John (155)
Carrilho da Graça, João Luís (186)
Castets, Simon (36, 191)
Castro, Raúl (83)
Cézanne, Paul (86)
Chan, Paul (138)
Cheng, Ian (129, 130)
Church, George (31, 72, 73)
Christo & Jeanne-Claude (50)
Churchill, Winston (82)
Cimabue (90)
Cixous, Hélène (42, 43)
Coluche (82)
Le Corbusier (157, 163)
Craig, Edward Gordon (57)
Craig-Martin, Michael (31)
Curiger, Bice (102)
Curtis, Adam (18, 19)
Dalí, Salvador (139)
Damisch, Hubert (185)
Davis, Miles (55)
De Kooning, Willem (99)
Deleuze, Gilles (95)
Denny, Simon (124, 125)
Derrida, Jacques (42)
Deutsch, David (74, 75)
Diamond, Jared (68, 69)
DiCaprio, Leonardo (121)
Duchamp, Marcel (118)
Eco, Umberto (33, 34, 40, 41)
Einstein, Albert (57)
Elíasson, Ólafur (45)
Ellis, Bret Easton (47)
Eno, Brian (156)
Enzensberger, Hans Magnus (185)
Fetisov, Valia (191)
Fiorentino, Rosso (90)
Fischli, Peter (118, 138, 152, 153)

FKA Twigs (80)
Freud, Sigmund (43)
Frey, Patrick (139)
Friðfinnsson , Hreinn (136, 137)
Fulton, Hamish (45)
Gad, Amira (124)
Gailhoustet, Renée (162, 163)
Gagliardi, Louisa (191)
García Lorca, Federico (161)
Giger, H. R. (138, 139)
Gilbert & George (161, 181)
Glissant, Édouard (11, 16, 21, 22)
Goldblatt, David (133)
Gonzalez-Foerster, Dominique (181)
Gonzalez-Torres, Felix (12)
Gordon, Douglas (119)
Green, Craig (167, 168)
Griffa, Giorgio (94, 95)
Hack, Jefferson (177)
Hadid, Zaha (158, 159)
Hamilton, Richard (150)
Hancock, Herbie (55)
Harari, Yuval Noah (174, 175)
Hawkins, Max (191)
Heidegger, Martin (43)
Hennings, Emmy (104)
Hiller, Holger (141)
Hirst, Damien (31)
Hockney, David (150)
Hoffmann, Luc (111, 112)
Hofmann, Albert (139)
Höller, Carsten (24)
Hon, Adrian (182)
Huxley, Aldous (183)
Iñárritu, Alejandro (121, 122)
Ireland, Patrick (92, 93)
Jacques, Juliet (180)
Jacquet, Jennifer (64, 65)
Jafa, Arthur (106, 107, 108)
Jeong A, Koo (13)
Jing, He (127, 128)
Jodorowsky, Alejandro (180)
Johnson, Philip (120)
Jonas, Joan (150)
Joyce, James (42)
Josephson, Mary (92)
Kafka, Franz (193)
Kahlil, Joseph (106)
Kandinsky, Wassily (103)
Kant, Immanuel (46)
Kessler, Harry (56, 57, 59)

Kierkegaard, Søren (46)
Klee, Paul (102, 187)
Kleeman, Alexandra (52, 53)
Knowles, Solange (107)
König, Kasper (148)
Koons, Jeff (14, 150)
Kubin, Alfred (139)
Kunz, Emma (102)
Lamar, Kendrick (106, 107)
Lassnig, Maria (147, 148, 150)
Latham, John (35, 36, 82)
Latour, Bruno (60, 61)
Ledoux, Claude-Nicolas (15)
Lem, Stanislaw (183)
Lerner, Ben (47, 48, 49, 177)
Locatelli, Gianantonio (117)
Lovecraft, H. P. (139)
Lubezki, Emmanuel (121, 122)
Maak, Niklas (162)
Macfarlane, Robert (46)
MacGregor, Neil (182)
Maginn, William (93)
Malevich, Kasimir (103, 158)
Mallett, Ronald (70)
Malraux, André (83)
Manzoni, Piero (118)
Marcelle, Cinthia (161)
McQueen, Steve (177)
Mead, Margaret (165)
Meireles, Cildo (161)
Melia, Felix (28)
Merz, Marisa & Mario (94)
Messager, Annette (25)
Messiaen, Olivier (157)
Metzger, Gustav (109, 110, 111, 113, 115)
Miessen, Markus (28)
Mingus, Charles (55)
Miyake, Akiko (70)
Mofokeng, Santu (133, 134, 135)
Mondrian, Piet (103)
Morton, Timothy (66, 67)
Mudekereza, Patrick (181)
Müller, Heiner (181)
Mustagab, Mohamed (132)
Musil, Robert (149)
Myles, Eileen (83)
Nakaya, Ukichiro (62)
Nasatir, Willa (24)
Nazareth, Paulo (45, 145, 146)
Nietzsche, Friedrich (161)

O'Doherty, Brian (92, 93)
Obama, Barack (107)
Oehlen, Albert (140, 141)
Ogi, Adolf (139)
Ondák, Roman (13)
Ono, Yoko (13)
Ovid (180)
Pariser, Eli (191)
Pärt, Arvo (80, 154)
Parreno, Philippe (19)
Paz, Octavio (83)
Peer, Madlaina (169)
Perec, Georges (27)
Peyton-Jones, Julia (12)
Pink Floyd (119, 120)
Pistoletto, Michelangelo (94)
Pliny the Elder (117)
Pollock, Jackson (99)
Poots, Alex (154)
Porter, Charlie (168)
Prada, Miuccia (169)
Price, Cedric (165)
Proust, Marcel (48, 193)
Rahm, Philippe (164, 165)
Rama, Edi (83)
Rathenau, Walther (57)
Rawsthorn, Alice (127)
Reich, Steve (155, 156)
Renaudie, Jean (163)
Richter, Gerhard (5, 17, 25, 80, 154, 155)
Rodchenko, Alexander (158)
Rodin, Auguste (63)
Van der Rohe, Mies (99)
Romagnoli, Lorenzo (77)
Rose, Rachel (119, 120, 177)
Rothko, Mark (99)
Ruf, Beatrix (95)
Sagan, Carl (176)
Schlingensief, Christoph (83)
Sehgal, Tino (45)
Sejima, Kazuyo (160)
Scott, Ridley (138)
Sharif, Hassan (104, 105)
Shawky, Wael (131, 132)
Shelley, Mary (66)
Shelley, Percy Bysshe (66)
Slominski, Andreas (118)
Smith, Patti (24)
Sonic Youth (154)
Soulages, Pierre (99, 100)

Spero, Nancy (31)
Spoerri, Daniel (13, 118)
Steiner, George (46)
Steiner, Rudolf (103)
Stephenson, Neal (81)
Sterling, Bruce (77, 78)
Steveni, Barbara (35, 82)
Stockhausen, Karlheinz (156)
Strauss, Richard (57)
Szeemann, Harald (145)
Tabane, Philip (54, 55)
Tarkovski, Andreï (11, 21)
Tatlin, Vladimir (158)
Thirlwell, Adam (192, 193)
Tiravanija, Rirkrit (119)
Titian (126)
Toroni, Niele (25, 26)
Trecartin, Ryan (33)
Trockel, Rosemarie (54, 150)
Ursprung, Philip (95)
Vasari, Giorgio (89, 90)
Van de Velde, Henry (57)
Walser, Robert (85, 140, 141)
Wedekind, Frank (104, 105)
West, Franz (25, 63)
West, Kanye (106, 107)
Xenakis, Iannis (156, 157)
Yiadom-Boakye, Lynette (170)
Venter, John Craig (31)
Da Vinci, Leonardo (10, 43)
Wales Bonner, Grace (166, 169, 170)
Weiss, David (118, 138, 152, 153, 159)
Williams, Pharrell (177)
Zambra, Alejandro (50, 51)
Zeilinger, Anton (70, 71)
Zweig, Stefan (17)

Index of Places

Abu Dhabi (85, 105, 159)
Africa (11, 145, 170)
Aix-en-Provence (86)
Albania (83)
Algeria (42)
Amsterdam (136, 137)
Antarctica (73)
Antilles (22)
Auckland (124)
Athens (157)
Baghdad (87, 159)
Basel (111, 146)
Beirut (85, 87, 88)
Berlin (23, 24, 59, 97, 104)
Belgium (31)
Brazil (45, 145, 160)
Cambridge (182)
Camargue (111, 112)
The Caribbean (11)
China (125, 127, 128)
Croydon (143)
Derry (92)
Doha (105)
Dresden (96, 98)
Dubai (104, 105)
Egypt (131)
Europe (23, 30, 42, 45, 46, 57, 94, 99, 147)
Estonia (155)
Florence (90)
France (31, 57, 59, 60, 82, 83, 100, 111, 143, 163, 164)
Fribourg (139)
Gais (140, 141)
Germany (57, 59, 83, 109, 115)
Granada (161)
Great Britain (58, 142)
Greenland (63)
Gruyère (139)
Guangzhou (159)

Hokkaido (62)
Hong Kong (125)
Innsbruck (24)
Ireland (31, 92)
Istanbul (187)
Italy (23, 31, 77, 90, 94, 188)
Japan (62, 70)
Jerusalem (174)
Johannesburg (133)
Kitakyushu (70)
Latin America (50, 160)
Lebanon (87)
London (28, 58, 69, 74, 119, 124, 143, 153, 158, 159, 160, 162, 166, 168, 182, 187)
Los Angeles (35, 74)
Lucerne (58)
Madrid (23)
Mamelodi (54)
Manchester (80, 154, 155)
Marseille (111)
Martinique (21)
Milan (23, 122, 150, 160)
Montpellier (99, 100, 111)
Montreux (55)
Munich (71)
Muralto (25)
New York (19, 24, 26, 45, 48, 55, 62, 63, 92, 99, 100, 104, 107, 120, 129, 140, 145, 148, 150)
New Zealand (124)
North Korea (31)
Oerlikon (139, 152)
Oxford (74, 174, 182)
Palma de Mallorca (71)
Papua New Guinea (69)
Paris (12, 13, 21, 23, 25, 28, 36, 42, 56, 60, 87, 104, 109, 157, 162, 163, 164, 177)
Persepolis (157)

Piacenza (117, 118)
Plauen (97)
Pompeii (119)
Portugal (186)
Pretoria (54)
Qatar (105)
Riehen (51)
Robben Island (134)
Rodez (99)
Rome (23, 158, 169)
São Paulo (160, 187)
San Francisco (86)
Seoul (106)
Sils Maria (161)
South Africa (54, 55, 133, 134)
Soweto (133)
St. Petersburg (93)
Switzerland (21, 25, 47, 55, 104,
    139, 140, 188)
Tenerife (71)
Thailand (31)
Turin (77, 94, 130)
United Arab Emirates (104)
United States (25, 83, 96, 99, 107,
    122, 150)
Venice (24)
Vienna (23, 147, 148, 149, 150, 159)
Vincennes (42)
Washington DC (187)
Weimar (56, 57)
Zurich (104, 118, 152, 191)

Editors
FINN CANONICA, CLÉMENT DIRIÉ

Editorial Coordination
CLÉMENT DIRIÉ, JESSICA BOURGOZ

Translation from the German
JUIDTH HAYWARD

Copyediting and Proofreading
CLARE MANCHESTER

Design
NICOLAS EIGENHEER/NICOLAS LEUBA,
Zurich

Color Separation and Print
MUSUMECI S.P.A., Quart (Aosta)

Typeface
HERMES-SANS (www.optimo.ch)

Drawings
All drawings by DAVID SHRIGLEY

Acknowledgments
CRISTINA BECHTLER, SVEN BEHRISCH,
ALICE RAWSTHORN

Printed in Europe

Published by

JRP|Ringier
Limmatstrasse 270
CH–8005 Zurich
T +41 (0) 43 311 27 50
E info@jrp-ringier.com
W www.jrp-ringier.com

ISBN 978-3-03764-510-9

JRP|Ringier books are available
internationally at selected
bookstores and from the following
distribution partners:

SWITZERLAND
AVA Verlagsauslieferung AG
Centralweg 16
CH–8910 Affoltern a.A.
avainfo@ava.ch
www.ava.ch

FRANCE
Les presses du réel
35 rue Colson, F-21000 Dijon
info@lespressesdureel.com
www.lespressesdureel.com

GERMANY AND AUSTRIA
Vice Versa Distribution GmbH
Postdamer Str. 93
D–10785 Berlin
info@viceversaartbooks.com
www.viceversaartbooks.com

UK AND OTHER EUROPEAN COUNTRIES
Cornerhouse Publications, HOME
2 Tony Wilson Place
UK–Manchester M15 4FN
publications@cornerhouse.org
www.cornerhousepublications.org

USA, CANADA , ASIA, AND AUSTRALIA
ARTBOOK|D.A.P.
75 Broad Street, Suite 630,
US–New York, NY 10004
order@dapinc.com
www.artbook.com

In the same series:

LIONEL BOVIER (ED.)
Vern Blosum (2014)
ISBN 978-3-03764-379-2

CLEMENT DIRIE (ED.)
Sheila Hicks: Apprentissages (2017)
ISBN 978-3-03764-483-6

JENS HOFFMANN
(Curating) From A to Z (2014)
ISBN 978-3-03764-372-3

JENS HOFFMANN
(Curating) From Z to A (2017)
ISBN 978-3-03764-509-3